365 More American English Idioms
An Idiom A Day

by
Michael DiGiacomo, MBA

Published in New York, USA June 2015

PLEASE!
DO NOT MAKE ILLEGAL COPIES OF THIS BOOK

To Gloria…who never gets tired of fixing my typos ☺

D1548293

A Message From Michael

Thank you for your interest in **365 More American English Idioms**. My first book of **365 American Idioms** was published in 2013 and due to popular demand, I am happy to present this latest book.

My name is **Michael DiGiacomo**, and I am a native New Yorker. I have been helping language students learn English since the early 1990's. I began my formal language-teaching career in Sendai, Japan in 1994. Since then, I have worked in the ESL field as an instructor, a teacher trainer, an academic director, and a language school director. In 2004, I earned an MBA in Global Management.

Now, I am the owner of **Happy English**, an English tutoring company in New York City. I teach students from all over the world both here in New York, and online in their country. Many of my students have given me inspiration for these lessons and this book grew out of some of those ideas.

I believe that language study should be both enjoyable and practical. In 2010, I started a website to provide a variety of English lessons to students all over the world. I set out to create lessons that were practical, easy to understand, and useful for self-study. In June of 2014, I started the **Happy English Podcast** to provide portable audio lessons for convenient English Study.

Idioms are commonly used in everyday, conversational English. I encourage you to study the lessons in this book, and begin using these phrasal verbs in your conversations. You will sound more natural when you do so.

As always, thanks for studying with me!

Find me online @ myhappyenglish.com

Table of contents

1: all along

Definition
from the beginning

Usage Notes
We usually use "know" with **all along**.

Structure
[someone] knows **all along** that ~

Examples
- Jack knew **all along** that the salesman was lying to him.
- I knew **all along** that trying to repair my computer would be difficult.

2: all the rage

Definition
widely popular

Usage Notes
We use **all the rage** when we talk about trends.

Structure
[something] is **all the rage**

Examples
- The hula-hoop was **all the rage** in the 1960's.
- Do you remember when the Rubik's Cube was **all the rage**?

3: as sick as dog

Definition
very sick; very ill

Usage Notes
In the old days people thought that dogs had viruses. When you are **as sick as a dog**, you're very sick.

Structure
[someone] is **as sick as a dog**

Examples
- I didn't go to work yesterday because I was **as sick as a dog**.
- Even though Randy was **as sick as a dog**, he still went to school.

4: at your wits' end

Definition
to have no more patience to endure a situation or person

Usage Notes
A person can be **at their wits' end** when they can no longer tolerate a particular person or situation

Structure
[someone] is **at their wits' end**

Examples
- I was **at my wits' end** when my flight was delayed for six hours, and then cancelled.
- I've tried everything to make her happy, but she is still not satisfied. I'm **at my wits' end**!

5: at the end of your rope

Definition
to be in a bad situation with no more options to resolve it

Usage Notes
A person can be **at the end of their rope** when facing a difficult sitiuation with no way to resolve it.

Structure
[someone] is **at the end of their rope**

Examples
- When my boss rejected my third proposal I was **at the end of my rope**.
- Jen was **at the end of her rope** when she ran out of gas on a deserted highway at 2am.

6: back to the drawing board

Definition
to start over from the beginning

Usage Notes
A person can be **back to the drawing board** when they realize their original plan is not good and needs to be revised. The subject can be either a person or it.

Structure
[someone] or [something] is **back to the drawing board**

Examples
- The boss rejected our proposal, so we are **back to the drawing board**.
- This marketing campaign was a total failure. It's **back to the drawing board**!

7: backseat driver

Definition
a passenger in a car who gives unwanted suggestions to the driver

Usage Notes
A person can be a **back seat driver** from any position in the car.

Structure
[someone] is a **back seat driver**

Examples
- I hate driving with Andy because he's a **backseat driver**.
- Stop being a **backseat driver**, dad. I know what I'm doing!

8: ballpark figure

Definition
an approximate amount or price

Usage Notes
A **ballpark figure** is an approximation given about a price, weight, distance, etc.

Structure
[something] is a **ballpark figure**

Examples
- Can you give me a **ballpark figure** about how long it will take to repair my car?
- I asked the tour guide for a **ballpark figure** and he said over 10,000 people a day visit this museum.

9: bark up the wrong tree

Definition
to be mistaken; to have the wrong idea

Usage Notes
This idiom comes from hunting, and refers to the action of a dog that mistakenly believes it's prey is in a particular tree. In such a case, the dog is **barking up the wrong tree**.

Structure
[someone] **barks up the wrong tree**

Examples
- Bob was **barking up the wrong tree** when he tried to ask Amy for a date. She only dates rich guys.
- You'll be **barking up the wrong tree** if you ask the boss for a raise. This company never gives raises.

10: basket case

Definition
to be very anxious or nervous about a certain situation

Usage Notes
A person who is a **basket case** is very nervous or anxious about something

Structure
[someone] is a **basket case**

Examples
- I was a **basket case** when I heard she was in a car accident.
- When Aaron found out he was getting fired, he was a **basket case**.

11: bat a thousand

Definition
to be very successful

Usage Notes
This idiom comes from the game of baseball where it means getting a hit at each turn at bat. A person who **bats a thousand** has continued or great success at something.

Structure
[someone] **bats a thousand**

Examples
- Wow! You made another sale! That's 25 sales today. You're **batting a thousand**!
- Every girl that Adam asks for a date says yes. He's **batting a thousand**.

12: be in the lap of luxury

Definition
to be in a luxurious situation

Usage Notes
If luxury a was a person, and that you sat in luxury's lap, you would be in a very luxurious situation.

Structure
[someone] is **in the lap of luxury**

Examples
- This hotel is first rate. I feel like I'm staying **in the lap of luxury**.
- Sitting in these leather seats, I'm **in the lap of luxury**.

13: bean counter

Definition
an accountant or finance officer in a company

Usage Notes
In the old days, beans had a high value and possibly, were treated like money.

Structure
[someone] is a **bean counter**

Examples
- Before we sign this contract, we need to make sure it is approved by the **bean counters**.
- The **bean counters** are working on next years' budget.

14: beat a dead horse

Definition
to waste effort repeatedly saying something that others are not interested in hearing

Usage Notes
When a person **beats a dead horse**, they either fruitlessly try to convince someone or annoyingly repeat something

Structure
[someone] **beats a dead horse**

Examples
- I will not buy that used car, so stop **beating a dead horse**. You don't need to continue telling me its merits.
- The first time you told that joke it wan't funny. Even thought you continue telling it, I still don't think it's funny, so please stop **beating a dead horse**!

15: beat around the bush

Definition
to speak indirecly in order to avoid saying the main point of an issue

Usage Notes
When a person **beats around the bush**, they intentionally avoid saying their main point.

Structure
[someone] **beats around the bush**

Examples
- Stop **beating around the bush** and tell me exactly. Do you love me or not!
- Sophia gets shy when she has to talk to the boss and often **beats around the bush**.

16: beat it

Definition
go away!

Usage Notes
Beat it is a very direct way of telling someone to leave or go away from you.

Structure
[stand-alone phrase]

Examples
- I'm trying to study, so just **beat it** ok? I want to be alone.
- I told the kids to **beat it** because I need some quite time to read my book.

17: beat someone to the punch

Definition
to do something before another person

Usage Notes
This idiom comes from boxing and means to punch your opponent before they hit you..

Structure
[someone] **beats** [another person] **to the punch**

Examples
- Ahmad tried to ask Karen for a date, but I **beat him to the punch**.
- You want to invent a digital music player? I think Apple **beat you to the punch**.

18: bend over backwards

Definition
to make every effort possible

Usage Notes
It takes a lot of effort for a person to bend over in a backwards direction. So, when you **bend over backwards**, you make a lot of effort for another's benefit.

Structure
[someone] **bends over backwards**

Examples
- I **bent over backwards** trying to solve my customer's problem. He appreciated my effort.
- I refuse to **bend over backwards** for Noah because he never shows any appreciation for anyyour help.

19: between a rock and a hard place

Definition
to be faced with two undesirable choices

Usage Notes
This idiom comes from an incident in the early 20th Century, when mine workers demanded better pay, but were told to keep working without a pay raise or quit. So the miners were between a rock (the mine shaft) and a hard place (poverty). When you are **between a rock and a hard place**, you are given two undesirable choices.

Structure
[someone] is **between a rock and a hard place**

Examples
- When the boss told us we would have either a 10% pay cut, or face a layoff, we were **between a rock and a hard place**.
- I'm **between a rock and a hard place**. If I go to the school dance with Emma, I will need to spend a lot of money. If I don't go, she will be angry with me.

20: big cheese

Definition
the important person in a company or organization

Usage Notes
Big means important. The focus of this idiom is the word big. We also use phrases like, the big guy, the big boss, and the big wheel.

Structure
[someone] is the **big cheese**

Examples
- The **big cheese** is going to come to our office from heaquarters today, so I need to wear a suit.
- I heard Olivia is having a meeting with the **big cheese** about her promotion. I hope it goes well.

21: big deal

Definition
an important issue

Usage Notes
When something is a **big deal**, it has significant importance.

Structure
[something] is a **big deal**

Examples
- Being invited to speak at our annual meeting is quite a **big deal** for Liam. All of the executives will be there.
- You'll be a half hour late? That's not a **big deal**. Drive carefully.

22: bigmouth

Definition
a person who talks too much, especially about gossip

Usage Notes
A person who is a **bigmouth** talks too much and often talks about gossip or something that was supposed to be a secret.

Structure
[someone] is a **bigmouth**

Examples
- Don't tell Jacob any of your personal secrets. He's a **bigmouth**.
- Isabella is such a **bigmouth**. She told everyone in the class that I like Emily.

23: blow

Definition
to lose; to miss an opportunity

Usage Notes
This use of the word blow is based on the definition of the word which means to explode. When something blows, it is destroyed. When you blow an an opportunity, it is likewise destroyed. Keep in mind, we say **blow**, **blew**, **blown**

Structure
[someone] **blows** [something]

Examples
- I'm studying hard because don't want to **blow** my exam.
- The guy **blew** the race when he crashed his car into the side wall of the track.

24: blow your own horn

Definition
to brag or boast

Usage Notes
Blowing a horn makes a lot of noise, and when a person boasts, they seem like they are making noise by **blowing their own horn**.

Structure
[someone] **blows** [their own] **horn**

Examples
- Mason was **blowing his own horn** during lunch, bragging about his new car.
- I'm sorry to **blow my own horn**, but I'm getting a promotion to manager!

25: blow off steam

Definition
to complain in order to release your stress

Usage Notes
This idiom alludes to an old-fashioned steam engine, which releases steam as a way of reducing its internal pressure.

Structure
[someone] **blows off steam**

Examples
- Thanks for listening to me complain. I needed to **blow off steam**.
- I heard what you said. Is that a real complaint, or were you just **blowing off steam**?

26: blow you away

Definition
to greatly impress a person

Usage Notes
The idiom **blow you away** means to amaze or shock you so much that it seems as if you are **blown away** by the wind.

Structure
[something] **blows** [someone] **away**

Examples
- Wow! Great concert! I was **blown away** by the singer.
- I have some big news. I think it will **blow** you **away**!

27: bomb

Definition
something amazing.

Usage Notes
A bomb is explosive and has a major impact. Likewise, when something is the **bomb**, it is amazing. On the other hand, like a bomb causes destruction, when something is a **bomb**, it is a failure. Be careful of "a" or "the" because they give this idiom the opposite meaning!

Structure
[something] is a **bomb** / the **bomb**

Examples
- That new Godzilla movie was a **bomb**! What a waste of time and money.
- The party last night was the **bomb**. I had a great time.

28: bombed

Definition
drunk

Usage Notes
A person who is drunk is **bombed**.

Structure
[someone] is **bombed**

Examples
- I was pretty **bombed** last night. I don't remember anything that I did at the party.
- Those guys are **bombed**. What are they drinking?

29: booked

Definition
completely filled / sold out

Usage Notes
This idiom is used mostly for hotels, and events. In the old days, hotels wrote the reservations in a book. Thus when a hotel or event is completely filled, we say the hotel or event is **booked**.

Structure
[something] is **booked**

Examples
- All of the hotels were **booked**, so we decided to go camping instead.
- My favorite restaurant was **booked** last night so I had to find a different place to have dinner.

30: boondocks / boonies

Definition
a rural area; the countryside

Usage Notes
This idiom is used to talk about rural places where people live.

Structure
the boondocks / the boonies

Examples
- My cousin lives in **the boondocks**. It's a nice area, but it takes about 30 minutes to reach the nearest store.
- I want to move to **the boonies** when I retire and live a quiet life away from the city.

31: booze

Definition
liquor; alcoholic drinks

Usage Notes
All types of alcoholic drinks can be considered to be booze

Structure
[uncountable noun]

Examples
- There was a lot of **booze** at the party last night. I think everyone was drunk.
- I can't drink anymore **booze**. I'll take a glass of water though.

32: bored to death

Definition
very bored

Usage Notes
When you feel very bored, you may feel as if you are so bored, that you have no more life inside. So, we say we are **bored to death**.

Structure
[someone] is **bored to death**

Examples
- I was **bored to death** at the meeting. The CEO spoke for three hours!
- I was **bored to death** when I saw that movie. It was not interesting at all.

33: brain

Definition
intelligent person

Usage Notes
A person who is a brain is so intelligent that their entire body is like a brain!

Structure
[someone] is **a brain**

Examples
- The new technician is quite **a brain**. He can fix anything, and do it very quickly.
- My sister is **a brain**. She can calculate in her head very quickly and accurately.

34: breadwinner

Definition
the family member who supports the family

Usage Notes
In the old days, bread was a basic food, so the person who wins the bread can feed the family.

Structure
[someone] is **the breadwinner**

Examples
- Ted's wife is **the breadwinner** in the family. She has a better job than he does.
- If **the breadwinner** in the family gets fired or laid off, the family will face difficult times.

35: break the bank

Definition
to overspend; to spend beyond the budget

Usage Notes
The bank represents the family budget and when you **break the bank**, you break the budget.

Structure
[someone] or [something] can **break the bank**

Examples
- I **broke the bank** on my last trip to Las Vegas.
- Last night's dinner at the steakhouse **broke the bank**. We'll need to eat at home the next few weekends.

36: break up with someone

to end a relationship with someone

Break means to destroy and when you **break up** a relationship, you destroy it. We usually use **break up with** when the direct object is used.

[someone] **breaks up** with [someone]

- I heard the receptionist **broke up with** her boyfriend. Now's your chance to date her!
- My cousin finally **broke up with** his weird girlfriend. He seems much happier now.

37: breath of fresh air

a refreshing change (of location, work, house, etc)

When you breathe fresh air you feel refreshed and good. So, when something is **a breath of fresh air**, you feel refreshed.

[something] is **a breath of fresh air**

- Quitting my job was like **a breath of fresh air**.
- Moving to this new apartment is like **a breath of fresh air**. I feel much more comfortable here.

38: bright and early

Definition
very early in the morning.

Usage Notes
The sunrise in the morning is bright, compared to the night sky and it happens early.

Structure
do [something] **bright and early**

Examples
- I woke up **bright and early** because I have an important meeting at 8am.
- We are taking a road trip this weekend, so we need to leave the house **bright and early** on Saturday.

39: brush up on

Definition
to refine or improve your skills

Usage Notes
You can **brush up on** some skill that you once were good at, but maybe haven't used in a while.

Structure
[someone] **brushes up on** [something]

Examples
- I need to **brush up on** my French before taking that trip to Paris.
- I guess I can play golf with you next month, but I think I should **brush up on** my swing before that.

40: burn someone up

Definition
to infuriate or anger someone

Usage Notes
When you are angry, it seems like your body temperature increases, like it is burning.

Structure
[something] **burns** [someone] **up**

Examples
- My boss won't let me take a day off on Friday. That **burns** me **up**.
- Paying extra for luggage at the airport really **burns** me **up**.

41: burn the midnight oil

Definition
to work or study well past midnight

Usage Notes
In the old days, oil lamps, which burned oil, were used to provide light at night.

Structure
[someone] **burns the midnight oil**

Examples
- We need to **burn the midnight oil** in order to finish this project.
- I was **burning the midnight** oil this week preparing for my exams.

42: butter up

Definition
to curry favor with or flatter someone in order to obtain something from them.

Usage Notes
Oil helps to make things work smoothly, and butter is a kind of sweet oil which makes smooth communication.

Structure
[someone] **butters up** [someone]

Examples
- I tried to **butter up** the boss but in the end, he refused to give me a day off.
- Don't try to **butter** me **up**. No matter what you say, you can't leave the office early today.

43: buy time

Definition
to delay doing something in order to improve your position or situation before doing it.

Usage Notes
When facing a deadline, some people wish to get more time.

Structure
[something] **buys** [someone] **time**

Examples
- I'm glad the meeting was postponed. That will **buy us time** to prepare a better presentation.
- Call the client and see if they can meet us on Friday instead of on Thursday. That will **buy us some** time.

44: buzzed

Definition
to be drunk (or high on drugs)

Usage Notes
Somone who is under the influence of alcohol may feel like they are flying, like a bee. Bees buzz in the air and that is the sound that they make.

Structure
[someone] is / gets **buzzed**

Examples
- Juan was pretty **buzzed** at the party last night
- Morgan is a light drinker and got **buzzed** after just one beer.

45: by word of mouth

Definition
from people talking about it

Usage Notes
When people talk, the words come from their mouth. This is how many businesses can grow - their customers talk to others about the business in a positive way.

Structure
[something] becomes known **by word of mouth**

Examples
- Sydney never advertised. She grew her business entirely **by word of mouth**
- The details of the grand opening of that business were spread **by word of mouth**.

46: call it a day (a night)

Definition
to verbally end an event (like work, a party, etc)

Usage Notes
Call it a day means "to say the day has ended." **Call it a night** means "to say the nighttime activity has ended."

Structure
Let's / Why don't we **call it a day/a night**

Examples
- It's late. Let's **call it a day** and finish painting the house tomorrow.
- I had a lot of fun tonight. Why don't we **call it a night**. It's already 3am!

47: can't stand

Definition
strongly dislike

Usage Notes
When you **can't stand** something or someone you strongly dislike it or them. This idiom is only used in the negative.

Structure
[someone] **can't stand** [someone] or [something]

Examples
- I **can't stand** to be in the same room with them.
- Peter **can't stand** his sister.

48: can't stomach

Definition
strongly dislike

Usage Notes
When you **can't stomach** something or someone you strongly dislike it or them.

Structure
[someone] **can't stomach** [someone] or [something]

Examples
- I just **can't stomach** that man.
- Lois **can't stomach** listening to the news.

49: catch your eye

Definition
to get your attention

Usage Notes
When you catch something, like a ball, you have it. When you catch an animal, you have it's complete attention. Similarly, when something or someone **catches your eye**, they have your complete attention.

Structure
[someone]/[something] **catches your eye**

Examples
- The woman at the end of the bar **caught my eye**.
- That lovely necklace in the showcase of the department store **caught my eye**.

50: caught dead (not be)

Definition
to never do something. This idiom is always used in a negative sentence.

Usage Notes
If you say you wouldn't be **caught dead** doing something, it means even if you were dead, you wouldn't do it.

Structure
[someone] wouldn't be **caught dead**

Examples
- I wouldn't be **caught dead** talking to Bob. I can't stand him.
- Jane said she wouldn't be **caught dead** wearing a dress like that. It's too flashy for her.

51: change your mind

Definition
to change your decision or opinion about something

Usage Notes
Your mind is the place where you make a decision or have an opinion.

Structure
[someone] **changes their mind**

Examples
- I was thinking of having pizza for lunch, but I **changed my mind**. I'm going to have salad instead.
- The boss **changed his mind** and decided to give everyone a bonus!

52: check out

Definition
to examine or investigate

Usage Notes
When you **check** something or someone **out**, you investigate in detail. We also use **check out** when we want to focus our attention on something.

Structure
[someone] **checks** a person or thing **out**

Examples
- I'm going to **check out** the new café. Do you want to join me?
- The boss asked me to **check out** his new smartphone. He can't receive any emails on it.

53: chicken (fraidy cat)

Definition
coward

Usage Notes
Perhaps a long time ago these animals were considered to be not brave.

Structure
[someone] is **a chicken / fraidy cat**

Examples
- Don't be a **fraidy cat**. Go ask Jane for a date.
- It seems like Sam won't ask the boss for a day off. He's a **chicken.**

54: chill out

Definition
to relax or calm down

Usage Notes
When you relax, you **chill out**. When someone is upset, you can tell them to **chill out**.

Structure
[someone] **chills out**

Examples
- We were **chilling out** at the bar last night because it was a tough day at the office.
- I know you're upset, but try to **chill out** a little. I'm sure your cat will come back home soon!

55: chip on your shoulder

Definition
to have a grievance or to hold anger about something.

Usage Notes
In the old days, when a person was angry with someone, they would put a wood chip on their shoulder. If the other person knocked it off, it meant that they were ready to fight.

Structure
[someone] **has a chip on their shoulder**.

Examples
- Danny seems to **have a chip on his shoulder**. I wonder what happened.
- Yes, I do **have a chip on my shoulder**. I am tired of you coming late to the office every day.

56: chocaholic

Definition
a person who loves to eat chocolate

Usage Notes
The "aholic" part of the word is a suffix meaning a lover of something (shopaholic, workaholic, pizzaholic, etc.) or an addiction to something (alcoholic).

Structure
[someone] is a **chocoholic**

Examples
- I'm a **chocoholic**. I eat a piece of chocolate every day.
- Ken is such a **chocoholic**, he even puts chocolate in his omlettes!

57: clear the air

Definition
to have a frank discussion in order to clarify a confused or tense situation

Usage Notes
When you are upset it is hard to breathe, just like when the air is not clean. So when you **clear the air**, you can breathe easier.

Structure
[someone] **clears the air**

Examples
- We've had a terrible misunderstanding, so I hope this meeting will **clear the air**.
- You need to **clear the air** with Luca. He's quite upset with you.

58: close shave

Definition
an almost dangerous situation

Usage Notes
Shaving can be dangerous, and **a close shave** can cause injury.

Structure
[something] is **a close shave**

Examples
- I had **a close shave** when I almost dropped my phone in the toilet!
- Bob and his girlfriend were at the same restaurant as Bob's wife and her mother. They didn't see each other, but that was **a close shave**.

59: come up with

Definition
to invent or create

Usage Notes
When you invent something or create a new way of doing something, you **come up with** it.

Structure
[somone] **comes up with** [something]

Examples
- I **came up with** a great way to cook asparagus.
- We need to **come up with** some new marketing ideas to sell more widgets.

60: couldn't care less

Definition
to not care

Usage Notes
If you really don't care about something (or someone), it would be impossible for you to care less about them. So we say you **couldn't care less** than you do now about them.

Structure
[someone] **couldn't care less** about [someone/something]

Examples
- My ex-girlfriend? I **couldn't care less** about her.
- I **couldn't care less** about football. I think it is a rediculous sport!

61: count on someone

Definition
to depend on

Usage Notes
When you depend on someone or something, you **count on it**.

Structure
[someone] **counts on** [someone/something]

Examples
- I am **counting on** my students to do their homework and study hard.
- Good luck on your business trip Hank. We are all **counting on** you to make the deal.

62: crazy about

Definition
to like or love something or someone very much

Usage Notes
When you like or love something or someone very much, you might do crazy things to show your love.

Structure
[someone] is **crazy about** [someone/something]

Examples
- Lori is **crazy about** lemon zest. She puts it on everything she eats!
- When Jen was a child, she was **crazy about** ice skating. Now she is just **crazy about** boys!

63: cream of the crop

Definition
the best of it's kind

Usage Notes
Cream is the best or richest part of milk. The **cream of the crop** is the best vegetable that the farmer grew.

Structure
[something] is **the cream of the crop**.

Examples
- This is my most popular book ever! It's **the cream of the crop**.
- The pizza at that restaurant is **the cream of the crop**.

64: crunch time

Definition
the most critical or important time, often near a deadline.

Usage Notes
Crunch means to make something smaller. **Crunch time** is when the amount of time available is seemingly less than what is needed.

Structure
[some situation] is **crunch time**

Examples
- There are only 5 minutes left in the game. Now, it's **crunch time**.
- We only have two more days before the new product launch. It's **crunch time**.

65: cut class

Definition
to illegally be absent from school

Usage Notes
When you **cut a class**, you are unofficially absent.

Structure
[someone] **cuts a class**

Examples
- Luke, why did you **cut** my **class** yesterday?
- Many high school seniors **cut class** in the spring time.

66: cut it out!

Definition
Stop it!

Usage Notes
When a movie director wants to stop the action in a scene, he yells cut. Here, cut means stop, so we use **cut it out** to mean stop.

Structure
[stand-alone phrase]

Examples
- You kids are being too loud. **Cut it out**.
- Lee, you have been drinking too much recently. **Cut it out** or I will leave you.

67: cut to the chase

Definition
to progress to the most important point

Usage Notes
When you want to (or want someone to) speak more directly and arrive at the main point quickly, we say **cut to the chase.**

Structure
[someone] **cuts to the chase**

Examples
- Let me **cut to the chase**. You've been late for work too many times. If it happens again, I have to fire you.
- We don't have much time left in this meeting. So **let's cut to the chase** and discuss the details of the contract.

68: dawn on

is realized or is finally understood

Usage Notes
Dawn happens suddenly when the sun starts to give light to the day. When something **dawns on** you, you suddenly think of it.

Structure
[something] **dawns on** [someone]

Examples
- It just **dawned on** me that we should look into expanding our business into Asia.
- Did that idea just **dawn on** you, or have you thought about it for a while?

69: days are numbered

Definition
there is not much time remaining

Usage Notes
This idiom means that the end of something is so clear, that we can count the days until it happens. When talking about people, it means they are in trouble.

Structure
[someone] or [something]'s **days are numbered**.

Examples
- My computer crashed again. I think its **days are numbered**.
- Jack, your **days are numbered**. If you come to work late once more you're going to be fired.

70: dead set against

Definition
completely against something

Usage Notes
Someone who is dead can not move, and if you are **dead set against** something, you can not and will not change your opinion.

Structure
[someone] is **dead set against** [something]

Examples
- The boss is **dead set against** permitting us to wear casual clothes in the office.
- My wife was **dead set against** the idea of taking a vacation this spring.

71: do the trick

Definition
to be the perfect solution

Usage Notes
A trick, like a magic trick, can do the job perfectly.

Structure
[something] **does the trick**

Examples
- It's very cold out, but this woolen hat will **do the trick** and keep me warm.
- I can replace the memory in your computer. That should **do the trick**. You won't have trouble anymore.

72: do up

Definition
do fasten (like a button) or set your hair

Usage Notes
The old fashioned word for a hairstyle is a hairdo, and do up comes from that.

Structure
[someone] **does up** [something]

Examples
- Jasper put on a suit and **did up** his hair. He looks good.
- **Do up** the buttons on your jacket before going out. It's very cold out there.

73: do your best

Definition
to perform as well as possible

Usage Notes
Your best is the best performance that you can do.

Structure
[someone] **does their best**

Examples
- I know this project will be difficult but I'll **do my b**est.
- I know you guys are **doing your best** and I appreciate your efforts.

74: dog-eat-dog

Definition
very competitve

Usage Notes
Dogs can be very competitive.

Structure
[something] is **dog-eat-dog**

Examples
- It's a **dog-eat-dog** world working on Wall Street these days. The competition is fierce
- Professional sports is a **dog-eat-dog** world. You need to be talented and have a strong desire to win.

75: double take

Definition
to look a second time in order to confirm.

Usage Notes
A double take is actually a double look at something.

Structure
[someone] does **a double take**

Examples
- When Phil saw his girlfriend in a café with another guy, he **did a double take** in disbelief.
- That guy looked just like Johnny Depp. It made me **do a double take**.

76: down for the count

Definition
to be completely finished, to lose, to be very tired

Usage Notes
This idiom comes from boxing. If the fallen boxer doesn't stand up after the count of ten, he has lost the match

Structure
[someone] is **down for the count**

Examples
- After running the race I was **down for the count**.
- I tried several times to get the customer to sign the contract, but he refused. It seems like I'm **down for the count**.

77: down in the dumps

Definition
feeling sad or depressed.

Usage Notes
The dump is where the garbage trucks drop off the trash. It is a very low place.

Structure
[someone] is **down in the dumps**

Examples
- Glen was **down in the dumps** when his girlfriend left him.
- You seem to be **down in the dumps**. Did anything bad happen today?

78: down the line

Definition
some time in the future; eventually.

Usage Notes
The line is a timeline, and **down the line** refers to some unknown point in time.

Structure
[something] is **down the line**

Examples
- I live in New York now, but **down the line** I'd like to move to Miami.
- ABC Co. has several branches in London now. Surely expanding all over the UK can happen **down the line**.

79: dress down (up)

Definition
To dress in fancy clothes (dress up) or very casual clothes (dress down).

Usage Notes
Dressing up means to wear nice or formal clothes and **dress down** means to wear more casual clothes

Structure
[someone] **dresses up** or **dresses down**

Examples
- Everyone in the office **dressed up** for the holiday party.
- I wear a suit to the office every day, so on the weekend I like to **dress down**.

80: drive you bananas (crazy)

Definition
to behave in a way that seriously bothers others

Usage Notes
Drive has the idea of moving with force or pressure.

Structure
[someone] or [something] **drives someone bananas / crazy**

Examples
- My neighbor plays loud music late at night. It **drives me bananas**.
- The boss always changing his mind **drives me crazy**. I wish he would make a decision and stick to it.

81: drop in the bucket

Definition
an insignificant amount of money.

Usage Notes
Among the potential amount of water a bucket can contain, a drop in the bucket is insignificant.

Structure
[something] is **a drop in the bucket**

Examples
- Dave is rich, so for him, buying a brand new car is **a drop in the bucket**.
- Buying a house isn't **a drop in the bucket**, so we need to make a decision carefully.

82: drop-dead gorgeous

Definition
extremely beautiful or attractive.

Usage Notes
This idiom gives us the idea that when we see a woman who is very beautiful, we are so amazed that we die.

Structure
[someone] is **drop-dead gorgeous**

Examples
- That actress is **drop-dead gorgeous**. I would love to meet her.
- Don't you think the new salewoman is **drop dead gorgeous**?

83: drum up

Definition
to gather; to collect; to assemble

Usage Notes
In the old days, people used drums to get the attention of others.

Structure
[someone] does something in order to **drum up** [something]

Examples
- I hope this new website will **drum up** business.
- Larry is trying to **drum up** support for his new marketing plan.

84: dump someone

to unexpectedly end a relationship with someone.

We use dump to mean "dispose of" something unwanted, like trash, old furniture, etc.

[someone] **dumps** [someone]

- Oliver finally **dumped** his weird girlfriend. Thank goodness!
- After twenty years of marriage, Yolanda **dumped** her husband for a younger man.

85: eager beaver

a very enthusiastic person

Beavers seem to work enthusiastically when they are building their dams.

[someone] is an **eager beaver**

- It seems like Rick is an **eager beaver** to finish this project.
- Kay is ready to work. She's quite an **eager beaver**.

86: face it

to admit to or accept something

When your face is pointed towards something, you need to deal with the thing that is in front of you.

[someone] **faces it**

- **Face it**, Mike. She loves another guy.
- I need to **face it**. I'm not getting any younger.

87: fair and square

fairly

A square is even on all sides.

[something] happens **fair and square**.

- I won the card game **fair and square**. Now, pay up!
- His offer looks **fair and square**. I think I'll accept it.

88: fall for

to fall in love

When you fall in love your body gets weak and feels like it will fall down. You **fall for** the other person.

[someone] **falls for** [someone]

- Lori and Nick **fell for** each other and soon they will get married!
- I **fell for** her the moment I looked into her eyes.

89: fat chance

impossible; no chance

A **fat chance** means that something is impossible, so the meaning seems to be opposite of the actual words.

[something] is a **fat chance**

- There is a **fat chance** that the boss will give us a raise, so don't bother asking him.
- You want me to walk from Central Park to Chinatown? **Fat chance**! I'm taking a bus.

90: feel free

Definition
do as you please, whenever you want to

Usage Notes
When you are free, you can do anything.

Structure
[someone] **feels free** to do [something]

Examples
- **Feel free** to call me if you have any questions or concerns.
- Kim said I should **feel free** to ask him for help anytime my PC breaks down.

91: first things first

Definition
we should do the important tasks first

Usage Notes
The thing that is first in a series should be done or come first.

Structure
[stand-alone phrase]

Examples
- **First things first**. Let's take the ingredients out of the fridge before we start cooking.
- You want to get married?! **First things first**. You should ask her for a date!

92: flat broke

Definition
having no money

Usage Notes
This idioms gives us the idea that the wallet is flat (no money inside) and broken (not working)

Structure
[someone] is **flat broke**

Examples
- We were **flat broke** the first year we got married.
- Lou is **flat broke**. He lost his job a year ago and has a lot of debit.

93: fly in the ointment

Definition
something interrupting the usual situation

Usage Notes
An ointment is an old fashioned word for medicine. If an insect got into the ointment, it would be spoiled.

Structure
[something] is **a fly in the ointment**

Examples
- The heavy rain was **a fly in the ointment** during yesterday's golf outing.
- I want to take a three-week vacation, but the company policy is **a fly in the ointment**.

94: fool around

Definition
not be serious

Usage Notes
A fool is not a serious person.

Structure
[someone] **fools around**

Examples
- Jay! Stop **fooling around**. Go finish your homework.
- Oscar spent the day **fooling around** instead of working.

95: for (in) a dog's age

Definition
for a long time

Usage Notes
One year for humans is about 7 years for a dog. So this idioms indicates it seems like a long time since something happened. We use **for a dog's age** & **in a dog's age**.

Structure
[something] hasn't happened **for/in a dog's age**

Examples
- I haven't seen my high school friends **for a dog's age**.
- I want to eat sushi. I haven't had it **in a dog's age**.

96: for the birds

useless, insignificant

Only small things are suitable for birds. We use this idiom to talk about things or ideas, etc, but not people.

[something] is **for the birds**

- This old cell phone is **for the birds**. I need a smartphone.
- The manager said that Fred's idea was **for the birds**. Poor Fred!

97: forty winks

a lot of sleep

When you wink many times, it appears that your eyes are closing, like you are sleepy.

[someone] has/gets **forty winks**

- I need to go home and get **forty winks**. I'm exhausted.
- I stopped driving for a while to get **forty winks**. I feel refreshed.

98: from day one

Definition
from the begining

Usage Notes
The first day that something happens is Day 1.

Structure
[something] happens from **day one**

Examples
- I haven't liked that guy **from day one**!
- **From day one** you have been bothering me. My answer is the same. I will not let you borrow my car!

99: from scratch

Definition
from basic ingredients

Usage Notes
This idioms means that something is cooked using basic ingredients; not instant food.

Structure
[something] is made **from scratch**

Examples
- I made this bread **from scratch**. It's so yummy!
- Do you make pasta sauce **from scratch**, or do you use the jar type?

100: full of it

Definition
lying

Usage Notes
It means lies and a person who is full of it is not telling the truth.

Structure
[someone] is **full of it**

Examples
- **You're full of it**. Johnny Depp was not shopping in Macy's this morning.
- I think Dan is **full of it**. He has a new car, so how could it break down this morning.

101: gathering dust

Definition
not being used

Usage Notes
When something in your house is not being used, it tends to collect dust, of course unless you clean it often.

Structure
[something] **gathers dust**

Examples
- My old cassette walkman is just **gathering dust** in my closet.
- Dave said his old textbooks are just **gathering dust**, so he's going to donate them to the school library.

102: get a load of

Definition
to notice; to observe

Usage Notes
A load is a large amount of something, so a load is easily noticable. When you get a load of something, you notice it. We usually use this idiom to make somone notice something.

Structure
Get a load of [something]

Examples
- **Get a load** of that guy. He's carrying two dogs! How cute!
- Did you **get a load** of Alice? She had her hair cut short!

103: get canned

Definition
to be fired; to lose your job

Usage Notes
In the old days, people would punish someone by hitting their buttocks, also called "the can" in slang. Getting fired is like getting kicked in the can by the boss.

Structure
[someone] **gets canned**

Examples
- Willy **got canned** because he was late too often.
- If you don't do your job properly, eventually you'll **get canned**.

104: get going

Definition
(1) to begin doing something; (2) to leave a place

Usage Notes
Get going has two meanings. (1) to start doing something (2) to leave.

Structure
[someone] or [something] **gets going**

Examples
- (1) The meeting **got going** as soon as the CEO arrived.
- (2) It's 11:30pm. I should **get going** so you can get some sleep!

105: get a handle on

Definition
to comprehend

Usage Notes
Holding the handle of a bag or pot gives you control of that item. When you **get a handle on** something you comprehend or understand it. We also use **have a handle on**.

Structure
[someone] **gets / has a handle** on something

Examples
- Ivan's explanation wasn't clear so it was hard to **get a handle on** what he wanted to say.
- After discussing the problem with everyone, I finally **have a handle on** what to do.

106: get it

Definition
to understand

Usage Notes
Get means receive and when you receive some information in your brain, you can understand it...you can **get it**.

Structure
[someone] **gets it**

Examples
- Sorry, I didn't **get it**. Can you explain it once more?
- **I get it**. So I just need to walk up three blocks and turn left. Thanks for the directions!

107: get lost

Definition
to lose your way

Usage Notes
Get means become, so when you **get lost** you become lost

Structure
[someone] **gets lost**

Examples
- I always **get lost** in Tokyo. There are so many train lines there.
- The streets in lower Manhattan are complicated, so it is easy to **get lost** there.

70

108: get off the ground

Definition
to begin doing something

Usage Notes
When an airplane gets off the ground it begins its journey. A project, a job, an idea, etc can **get off the ground**.

Structure
[something] **gets off the ground** or [someone] gets [something] off the ground.

Examples
- I've finally gotten my research **project off the ground**. I hope to finish it withing two months.
- Because of a lot of company politics, it is difficult to **get** new projects **off the ground** here.

109: get on your back

Definition
to annoy or bother somone

Usage Notes
If a person jumps on your back, you would be greatly bothered by it. We use **get** or **be on someone's back**.

Structure
[someone] **gets on someone's back**

Examples
- Ryo's boss **is always on his back**. He hates it!
- Chris said his wife **got on his back** because she wants to buy new livingroom furniture.

110: get plastered

Definition
to get drunk

Usage Notes
Plaster is flat on a wall, like a drunk person who needs the wall's help in order to stand up.

Structure
[someone] **gets** (or is) **plastered**

Examples
- Everyone **got plastered** at Jerry's party last night
- You **were** pretty **plastered** at dinner last night. How do you feel today?

111: get rid of

Definition
to dispose of something

Usage Notes
We use **get rid of** to mean both dispose of something in the trash, or to give something away so that you don't have it anymore

Structure
[someone] **gets rid of something**

Examples
- We **got rid of** twenty boxes of garbage when we moved to the new apartment.
- I want to **get rid of** my old bicycle. If you know anyone who wants it, they can have it free!

112: get something straight

Definition
to explain

Usage Notes
When you **get something straight**, you explain it clearly in order to avoid any misunderstanding or confusion. We often use, **let me get something straight**.

Structure
[someone] gets something straight.

Examples
- **Let me get something straight**. I like Fey, but I'm not in love with her.
- **Let's get something straight**. The rule is you need to start work at 9. If you are late again, you'll get fired.

113: get the ball rolling

Definition
to begin something

Usage Notes
To start a game like bowling or billiards, you roll the ball.

Structure
[someone] **gets the ball rolling**

Examples
- Don, we are a week late in starting the project. Let's **get the ball rolling**.
- Now that we have decided the work team, we can **get the ball rolling** on this project.

114: get the hang of something

Definition
to get used to something or doing something

Usage Notes
When you can finally do something, you **get the hang of it**.

Structure
[someone] **gets the hang of** something

Examples
- With some practice, I finally **got the hang of** skateboarding.
- I'll never **get the hang of** driving in snow.

115: get the show on the road

Definition
to begin an event

Usage Notes
In the old days, a show would travel around the country. When you **get the show on the road**, you begin doing it.

Structure
[someone] **gets the show on the road**

Examples
- The plane leaves in one hour, let's **get the show on the road**.
- You're late again, Jimmy, **get the show on the road** and get ready for school.

74

116: get something under your belt

Definition
to become good at doing something

Usage Notes
Your belt is very close to you so when you **get something under your belt**, you know it well.

Structure
[someone] **gets/has** [something] **under their belt**

Examples
- Once I **get this** practice test **under my belt**, I'll be ready for the final exam.
- Tom is a master builder, so he has a lot of experience **under his belt**.

117: get your hopes up

Definition
to have feelings of high expectation and excitement about something

Usage Notes
When you **get your hopes up** you get very excited and have a lot of hope for that thing.

Structure
[someone] **gets their hopes up**

Examples
- Don't **get your hopes up**, Sally won't go to the dance with you.
- The interview went well, I've **got my hopes up** for this job.

118: ghost of a chance

Definition
only a slight chance

Usage Notes
A ghost is almost invisible so are **ghost of a chance** is only a slight chance.

Structure
[someone] has **a ghost of a chance**

Examples
- I don't have **a ghost of a chance** to win the lottery.
- I don't have **a ghost of a chance** to get a date with Amy.

119: give it a shot

Definition
to try

Usage Notes
When you **give something a shot**, you try it with not much preparation.

Structure
[someone] **gives something a shot**

Examples
- You can do that, go ahead, **give it a shot**.
- I've never cooked meatloaf. I think I'll **give it a shot** tonight.

120: give it rest

stop doing something that annoys others

When you **give a something a rest** you stop doing it.

[stand-alone phrase]

- **Give it a rest**, Mary. We're not going to the candy store so please stop asking me.
- That drumming has given me a headache. Please, **give it a rest**.

121: give me a break

don't be so harsh

We usually ask someone to **give us a break** we were having a hard time doing something.

[stand-alone phrase]

- I've listened to your complaints all day. Please! **Give me a break**!
- I asked my teacher to **give me a break** and let me turn in my homework late, but he said no.

122: give you the creeps

Definition
to make one feel uncomfortable

Usage Notes
The creeps is an uncomfortable feeling. We say that someone or something **gives us the creeps**.

Structure
[something or someone] **gives** [someone] **the creeps**

Examples
- That strange man is staring at me. He **gives me the creeps**.
- Spiders **give Mary the creeps**.

123: give you the ax

Definition
to fire; to terminate employment

Usage Notes
An axe can cut something. When someone is fired from their job, we can say the company cut them, so we say the company **gives them the axe**.

Structure
[someone] **gives** [someone] **the axe**

Examples
- The factory **gave ten people the axe** today because of budget cuts.
- Kathy, you've been late everyday this week. I have no choice but to **give you the axe**.

78

124: give you the cold shoulder

Definition
to ignore someone

Usage Notes
When you are upset with someone, you may turn your body away from them so that your shoulder points towards them. Your shoulder represents your cold attitude.

Structure
[someone] **gives** [someone] **the cold shoulder**

Examples
- Frank **gave me the cold shoulder** at the meeting today. I wonder why he is upset.
- When Kris **gave her ex-boyfriend the cold shoulder** at the party, the mood became dark for everyone.

125: give you the time of day

Definition
to be curt with others

Usage Notes
We usually use this idiom to complain about a busy person, someone who is so busy they don't have the time to tell someone the time.

Structure
[someone] doesn't give someone the time of day

Examples
- The boss is so busy, he can't **give me the time of day**.
- There is no use talking to Mike. That guy can't even give **you the time of day**.

126: give up

Definition
to acquiesce

Usage Notes
When you **give up** you don't do something anymore.

Structure
[someone] **gives up**

Examples
- I can't figure out what to do any more. I **give up**.
- I looked for my lost keys all morning and finally **gave up**.

127: give you static

Definition
to complain to someone

Usage Notes
Static is the noise between the radio stations. Many people find that noise to be annoying. When someone **gives you static** they bother you about something.

Structure
[someone] **gives** [someone] **static**

Examples
- Mom will **give you static** if you don't clean your room.
- I need to be on time today. My boss will **give me static** if I'm late again.

128: go by the book

Definition
to follow the rules exactly

Usage Notes
Generally, rules are written down, like in a book. When you **go by the book**, it gives us the image of doing something while reading the rule book or according to the book.

Structure
[someone] **goes by the book**

Examples
- The manager isn't flexible. He always **goes by the book**.
- When a bank lends money it always **goes by the book**.

129: go crazy (nuts)

Definition
to enjoy something very much

Usage Notes
Someone who **goes crazy** or **goes nuts** enjoy something very much. We use **goes crazy/nuts over** when the direct object is used.

Structure
[someone] **goes crazy/nuts**

Examples
- I **go nuts over** rock music.
- It's finally the weekend. Time to **go crazy** and have fun.

130: go for a spin

Definition
to test-drive a car

Usage Notes
When the wheels of a car spin, the car moves.

Structure
[someone] **goes for a spin**

Examples
- We **went for a spin** in a new sports car.
- The mechanic **went for a spin** around the block to check the car's new brakes.

131: go into business

Definition
to open your own company

Usage Notes
When you **go into business** you start your own business,

Structure
[someone] **goes into business**

Examples
- I'm going to **go into business** and open a dress shop.
- After Bill graduated, he **went into business** with his father.

132: go off the deep end

Definition
to react irrationally

Usage Notes
The deep end means the deep end of the swimming pool. It would be irrational for a person who is a beginning swimmer to go into the deep end of the pool.

Structure
[someone] **goes off the deep end**

Examples
- All of the stress of her divorce caused her to **go off the deep end**.
- Don't **go off the deep end** and start crying again.

133: go out on a limb

Definition
to do something that is a little risky.

Usage Notes
A limb is the branch of a tree and sometimes going out on the tree branch can be dangerous or risky.

Structure
[someone] **goes out on a alimb**

Examples
- I'm going to **go out on a limb** and spend my last dollar on a lottery ticket.
- Fred **went out on a limb** to open his own café, but in the end he made a fortune.

134: go over like a lead balloon

Definition
to completely fail

Usage Notes
Lead is a very heavy metal. A balloon that is made of lead would not fly and would basically be a failure.

Structure
[something] **goes over like a lead baloon**

Examples
- That comedian's joke's were not funny and **went over like a lead balloon**.
- Peter's suggestion **went over like a lead balloon**. It's clear that he has no business sense.

135: go overboard

Definition
do act or do excessively

Usage Notes
Overboard means over the side of the ship, and going overboard in the sea would be an excessive or extreme act.

Structure
[someone] **goes overboard**

Examples
- Sue will **go overboard** on her boyfriend's birthday party. She hired a magician!
- Don't **go overboard** with all that makeup. You'll look like a clown!

136: go through the roof

Definition
to become very angry

Usage Notes
When you react in a surprising way you pick your head up, so we have the image of your head going through the roof.

Structure
[someone] **goes throught the roof**

Examples
- When dad finds out about the car accident, he'll **go through the roof**.
- If the cost of gasoline keeps rising, food prices will **go through the roof**.

137: go with the flow

Definition
to deal with and accept adversity

Usage Notes
When you're on the river the water flows in one direction, so when you **go with the flow** of the water, you follow that direction.

Structure
[someone] **goes with the flow**

Examples
- The boss wants everyone to work on Sunday, so I guess I should also **go with the flow**.
- I made my sales pitch, so now I just need to **go with the flow** and see how the customers react.

138: good for you

Definition
That's good news!

Usage Notes
Something that is **good for you** has benefit for you. You can also use **good for him**, **good for her**, etc.

Structure
[stand-alone phrase]

Examples
- You got a promotion and a raise? **Good for you**!
- I heard Jack was finally made captain of the soccer team. **Good for him**!

139: goose is cooked

Definition
to be in trouble

Usage Notes
When a goose is cooked that signals the end of it's life, which is not a good situation for the goose.

Structure
[someone]'s **goose is cooked**

Examples
- My **goose is cooked**, I failed the math test.
- If mom finds out about the broken window, **my goose is cooked**.

140: grab something

Definition
to get / to have / to buy

Usage Notes
Grab can be used in casual English to mean **get** or **have** or **ride**.

Structure
[someone] **grabs** [something]

Examples
- Let's **grab** a beer after work tonight.
- I'm going to **grab** dinner on my way home from work.

141: greasy spoon

Definition
an old fashioned and not so clean restaurant surving home-style cooking

Usage Notes
An old dirty restaurant probably has some greasy spoons, forks, or knives, etc.

Structure
[restaurant name] is a **greasy spoon**

Examples
- No way will I eat there, that restaurant is a **greasy spoon**.
- The truck driver stopped at the nearest **greasy spoon** for some breakfast.

142: green light

Definition
approval to do something

Usage Notes
When driving, a green light means go. We generally use this idiom with "the" - **the green light.**

Structure
[someone] has or gets **the green light.**

Examples
- We finally **got the green light** to open a branch office in Seoul.
- There is no way your wife will **give you the green light** to go to Las Vegas with your friends!

143: gung ho

Definition
enthusiastic

Usage Notes
Gung ho is the English pronunciation of a Chinese word which means to work together. This word was used by American Marines in World War II.

Structure
[someone] is **gung ho**

Examples
- Mary was **gung ho** about the project.
- Steven's **gung ho** attitude helped get him a promotion.

144: had it up to here

to endure something to your limit

Usage Notes
In this idiom, "here" represents the top of a container which is filled. This is the limit of the container, and it shows the limit of a person to endure something.

Structure
[someone] has had it up to here

Examples
- I've **had it up to here** with your coming to work late. You're fired.
- George has **had it up to here** with that dog barking all night. He called the police and complained.

145: hands are tied

Definition
to be unable to change a situation because of certain rules or policies

Usage Notes
If someone ties your hands together you would be unable to do anything.

Structure
[someone]'s **hands are tied**

Examples
- I'd like to give you a bonus, but my **hands are tied**. The company policy doesn't allow bonuses anymore.
- Because of the the rules and regulations about lending money, the banker's **hands were tied**.

146: hang in there

Definition
Don't give up! Be patient!

Usage Notes
You can imagine somebody hanging from a rock after a mountain climbing accident. His friend would say, "continue hanging there until help arrives and don't give up!"

Structure
[stand-alone phrase]

Examples
- I know you feel sad that your boyfriend left you, but **hang in there**. You'll find a better guy soon, I'm sure!
- I know I can finish my homework if I just **hang in there**.

147: hang out

Definition
to spend relaxing time

Usage Notes
We used to **hang out** to mean spend relaxing time.

Structure
[someone] **hangs out**

Examples
- I like to **hang out** with my friends in the park.
- Sometimes we go dancing, and sometimes we just **hang out** at home.

148: happy camper

Definition
a person who is in a good mood

Usage Notes
People often have an enjoyable time when they go camping, so a **happy camper** is a person who is in a good mood.

Structure
[someone] is a **happy camper**

Examples
- Sal is a **happy camper.** He finally got a new TV.
- A long nap in the afternoon made the baby a **happy camper**.

149: have a blast

Definition
to enjoy very much

Usage Notes
A blast is an explosion, so when you have a blast, you have an explosion of enjoyment.

Structure
[someone] **has a blast**

Examples
- I went to a party last night and I **had a blast**.
- Dad gave us some pocket money and told us to **have a blast** at the amusement park.

150: have a screw loose

Definition
to be crazy

Usage Notes
If there is a loose screw in a machine it won't work properly. This idiom lets us imagine our brain is a machine and if there is a loose screw in your "machine brain" it also won't work properly.

Structure
[someone] **has a screw loose**

Examples
- Leo's been acting crazy. I think **he has a screw loose**.
- Jack must **have a screw loose.** He ran right into the street without looking both ways.

151: have an axe to grind

Definition
to have a complaint against someone

Usage Notes
You grind an axe on its sharpening stone which makes a lot of noise. We use **have an axe to grind with** when a direct object is used.

Structure
[someone] **has an axe to grind**

Examples
- Yes, I **have an axe to grind**! Jeff stole my girlfriend.
- I **have an axe to grind** with you about today's meeting.

152: have an eye on

Definition
to observe something or someone who may be/do wrong

Usage Notes
When you **have your eye on** something or someone you observed very carefully.

Structure
[someone] **has an eye on** [something/someone]

Examples
- I **have an eye on** that suspicious looking guy.
- I **have an eye on** the baby all day. Now that he is crawling, I have to watch everthing he does.

153: have it made

Definition
to be in a very good life situation, especially financially.

Usage Notes
Here, "it" represents life and when you have it made, you are in a good life situation.

Structure
[someone] **has it made**

Examples
- Jenny **has it made**. She's married to a very rich lawyer.
- If I win the lottery, I'll **have it made**.

154: have my back against the wall

Definition
to be in a difficult situation without a way out

Usage Notes
When your back is against the wall, you can not move anymore.

Structure
[someone] **has their back against the wall**

Examples
- My term paper is due tomorrow, and I haven't started it. I **have my back against the wall**.
- The rent is due and I have no money. I really **have my back against the wall**.

155: have your heart set on

Definition
to have very high expectations about something.

Usage Notes
Your feelings of hope lie in your heart, so when you have your heart set on something, you have your feelings set on that thing.

Structure
[someone] has their **heart set on something**

Examples
- I really **have my heart set on** chocolate ice cream.
- Jenny had **her heart set on** that trip to Disneyland.

94

156: head start

Definition
the chance to start something ahead of schedule.

Usage Notes
Head is short for ahead, which means in front. So when you have a head start, you start ahead of others.

Structure
[someone] has a **head start**

Examples
- Today, I got to the office early and got a **head start** on my work.
- Ralph got a **head start** on the others and arrived at the hotel before them.

157: hear someone out

Definition
to listen to someone carefully

Usage Notes
Here, "out" means outside of your opinion, so when you **hear** someone **out**, you listen to them completely without interjecting your opinion.

Structure
[someone] **hears** [someone/something] **out**

Examples
- I want you to listen to me, and **hear me out** with my plan
- I know you think my story is an excuse, but please **hear me out**.

158: history

something that is no longer relavent

History is what happened before, often a long time ago and some history has no relevance to the present. This idiom shows that something is like forgotten history.

[someone] or [something] is **history**

- I'm not dating him anymore. We're **history**!
- Poodle skirts and saddle shoes are not in style. They're **history**.

159: hit the nail on the head

to be exactly correct

In carpentry, when you hit a nail on its head with a hammer, your hammering skill is precise and exact.

[someone] **hits the nail on the head**

- Yesterday, I answered the question correctly, and **hit the nail on the head**.
- Tommy **hit the nail on the head** when he solved the mystery.

160: hit the road

Definition
to leave

Usage Notes
When your feet (or the feet of your horse) hit the road, the journey begins with that first step.

Structure
[someone] hits the road

Examples
- I'm leaving on vacation. Time to **hit the road**.
- I'm going to **hit the road** at 6:00 tonight.

161: hit the town

Definition
to enjoy the nightlife in a city

Usage Notes
Here, hit means go, so when you **hit the town**, you go to the night spots there.

Structure
[someone] **hits the town**

Examples
- Tonight we're going to **hit the town** and party!
- Let's **hit the town** tonight. I feel like dancing.

162: hold out (for)

to wait patiently for a better opportunity

We use **hold out** as a verb, but it is possible to use **hold out** as a noun to describe a person who keeps their opinion strong even though others have given up.

[someone] **holds out for** [something]

- That job didn't pay enough. I'm going to **hold out for** a better offer.
- Ben was the only **hold out**. Everyone else in the office voted yes to the plan.

163: hold your liquor

to be able drink alcohol responsibly and not get too drunk

If you can **hold your liquor**, you can drink a lot of alcohol without getting sick or acting irresponsibly.

[someone] **holds their liquor**

- If you can't **hold your liquor**, you might end up in trouble.
- When you drink with sailors, you better be able to **hold your liquor**.

164: hold your tongue

Definition

to refrain from speaking when you really want to say something.

Usage Notes

You need to use your tongue when you speak, so when you hold your tongue, you can't speak.

Structure

[someone] **holds their tongue**

Examples

- If you don't have something nice to say, it's better to **hold your tongue**.
- Mary could not **hold her tongue** and had to say her honest opinion about Donna's new shoes.

165: hot and bothered

Definition

upset and angry

Usage Notes

When you get upset, your body temperature tends to increase, and being upset bothers your usual life.

Structure

[someone] is hot and bothered

Examples

- Frank's comment left me **hot and bothered**.
- Bill gets **hot and bothered** when someone sits in his chair.

166: hot topic

Definition
an issue or news story that many people are talking about

Usage Notes
In this idiom, "hot" has the meaning of popular or very fresh, like hot bread from the oven.

Structure
[something] is a **hot topic**

Examples
- Today's **hot topic** is that new rock band.
- The presidential debate is always a **hot topic**.

167: hothead

Definition
a person who easily gets angry

Usage Notes
Getting angry causes your temperature to go up, especially in your head.

Structure
[someone] is a **hothead**

Examples
- Kim yells at everyone. She's such a **hothead**.
- Calm down, don't be such a **hothead**.

168: if the shoe fits, wear it

Definition
if the situation pertains to you, then you should accept it.

Usage Notes
This is an analogy to shoes. Shoes that fit are perfect for you.

Structure
[stand-alone phrase]

Examples
- The teacher said no talking during class. **If the shoe fits, wear it**.
- Yesterday we were saying people need to be nicer to each other. **If the shoe fits, wear it**.

169: in a stew

Definition
in a bad mood

Usage Notes
Stew is cooked for a long time and when you are stewed, you are in a bad mood for long time.

Structure
[someone] is/gets **in a stew**

Examples
- Bobby is **in a stew** over next week's math exam.
- Don't get **in a stew** over your tax bill. Just pay it and forget it.

170: in any case

Definition
no matter what the situation

Usage Notes
Here, case means situation, so **in any case** means no matter what the situation or regardless of the situation.

Structure
[stand-alone phrase]

Examples
- I don't know what the weather will be like tomorrow. **In any case,** I will go to the park.
- I'm not sure if I will drive or take the bus. **In any case**, I'll be at your house by noon.

171: in charge of

Definition
responsible for

Usage Notes
Charge means entrust, thus **in charge** of means entrusted in or responsible for

Structure
[someone] is **in charge of** [something]

Examples
- Nancy was **in charge of** the class picnic.
- The new manager is **in charge of** the factory and the warehouse.

172: in good hands

Definition
in a safe situation

Usage Notes
Someone who has good hands is capable, so when you are **in good hands,** someone is quite capable of helping you.

Structure
[someone] is **in good hands**

Examples
- Larry knows what he's doing. You're **in good hands**.
- I know my car is **in good hands** when I go to that mechanic.

173: in good spirits

Definition
felling happy or well

Usage Notes
Your spirit is your mood so when you are **in good spirits** you are in a good mood.

Structure
[someone] is **in good spirits**

Examples
- Ned got some good news this morning. He's **in good spirits**.
- A sunny day always puts me i**n good spirits**.

174: in no time

Definition
shortly; soon; in just a little while

Usage Notes
No time means zero time, so **in no time** means very shortly.

Structure
[something] happens **in no time**

Examples
- I'll have that answer for you **in no time**.
- Yolanda got back from the store **in no time**.

175: in person

Definition
face to face, as opposed to on TV or virtually

Usage Notes
When you meet somebody **in person** you meet them face-to-face.

Structure
[someone] meets [someone] **in person**

Examples
- I met that TV star **in person** at the mall.
- I have to appear **in person** at the trial.

176: in progress

Definition
currently being worked on

Usage Notes
When you do something you make progress, so something that is **in progress** is currently being done.

Structure
[something] is **in progress**

Examples
- My painting isn't finished yet. It's a work **in progress**.
- With all the construction **in progress**, the traffic is horrible.

177: in seventh heaven

Definition
feeling very elated

Usage Notes
The number **seven** rhymes with the word **heaven** and heaven is a happy place.

Structure
[someone] is **in seventh heaven**

Examples
- I'm **in seventh heaven** when my cousins visit.
- A vacation always puts me **in seventh heaven**.

178: in the doghouse

Definition
in trouble, usually with a spouse or boss

Usage Notes
The dog lives outside in the doghouse, and if you are in trouble with your spouse or boss they may send you out to the doghouse too!

Structure
[someone] is **in the doghouse**

Examples
- Harry was **in the doghouse** because he came home late.
- Sarah will be **in the doghouse** at work if she doesn't finish that presentation.

179: in the driver's seat

Definition
in charge or responsible for something

Usage Notes
The driver is the responsible person in the car, so when you are **in the drivers seat** you are responsible.

Structure
[someone] is **in the driver's seat**

Examples
- I made the best offer on that house. I'm **in the driver's seat**.
- Since Ellen was the boss, she was **in the driver's seat** at the meeting.

180: in the mood

Definition
desiring something

Usage Notes
Your mood is your feeling and when you feel like something, you are **in the mood** for it.

Structure
[someone] is **in the mood**

Examples
- Im **in the mood** for some jazz. Let's go out to night.
- I'm **in the mood** for an ice cream sundae.

181: in the nick of time

Definition
just in time; just before the deadline

Usage Notes
A nick is a notch or a small cut, which represents one second of time.

Structure
[something] happens **in the nick of time**

Examples
- The police arrived **in the nick of time**.
- **In the nick of time**, the ambulance reached her house and took her to the hospital.

182: in your / that neck of the woods

Definition
in your neighborhood; your town

Usage Notes
A neck is the narrow part of something. The narrow part of the woods would be a good place to build a house.

Structure
[someone] or [something] is **in your neck of the woods**

Examples
- So, what's new **in your neck of the woods.**
- I've never been in **that neck of the woods**. Is it nice there?

183: into something

Definition
a fan of; enjoy doing

Usage Notes
When you are **into something** you really enjoyed doing that or like it very much.

Structure
[someone] is **into** [something]

Examples
- Vera goes to the gym every day. She's really **into** fitness.
- I'm **into** astrology. What's your sign?

184: it's a deal

Definition
we both agree

Usage Notes
A deal is a negotiation, so when you say **it's a deal**, it means both people agree.

Structure
[stand-alone phrase]

Examples
- **It's a deal**. I'll bring the soda, you bring the chips.
- So we agree on the price? OK, **it's a deal**.

185: it's in the bag

Definition
a sure victory or sure success

Usage Notes
When you buy something they usually put it in the bag. The bag signifies the end of a successful transaction. So when something is **in the bag** it's a certain success.

Structure
[something] **is in the bag**

Examples
- I'm pretty sure about that promotion. **It's in the bag**.
- With Mike on our team, winning the game is **in the bag**.

186: jump at the chance

Definition
do take action without any hesitation

Usage Notes
If you have the opportunity to do something you may move quickly or act quickly. When you **jump at the chance** you take quick action without hesitation.

Structure
[someone] **jumps at the chance** to do something

Examples
- I'd **jump at the chance** to go into space.
- Jeff would **jump at the chance** to visit New York.

187: jump the gun

Definition
to act prematurely

Usage Notes
A gun is used to start the race. A person who **jumps the gun** starts the race before the gun is shot.

Structure
[someone] **jumps the gun**

Examples
- Don't **jump the gun** and go home early without getting permission from the boss.
- If you **jump the gun**, you will be disqualified from the race.

188: jump to conclusions

Definition
to assume the facts of a situation prematurely

Usage Notes
Here, jump means to rush or move quickly. When you **jump to conclusions**, you assume what the situation is prematurely.

Structure
[someone] **jumps to conclusions**

Examples
- Don't **jump to conclusions** and say he was wrong. You need to hear both sides of the story.
- If you **jump to conclusions**, you may not hear the truth.

189: just what the doctor ordered

Definition
the perfect thing for this situation

Usage Notes
A doctor can order medicine for you, so something that is **just what the doctor ordered** is exactly what you need.

Structure
[something] is **just what the doctor ordered**

Examples
- This cold glass of water is **just what the doctor ordered**.
- Ah, a weekend with no yard work. That is **just what the doctor ordered**.

190: keep an eye out

Definition
to be observant

Usage Notes
When you keep your eye looking out of your head, you are being observant.

Structure
[someone] **keeps an eye out**

Examples
- **Keep an eye out** for the postman. I am expecting a package.
- I will **keep an eye out** for a sale on blankets. I need a new one.

191: keep in touch with

Definition
to remain in contact with someone

Usage Notes
When you keep in touch with someone you stay within range of touching them. In other words you keep in contact with them. We use **keep in touch** or **stay in touch**.

Structure
[someone] **keeps/stays in touch with** [someone]

Examples
- Even though school is out, I will **keep in touch** with my roomate.
- I promised to **stay in touch** with my cousin in Greece.

192: keep it up

to continue

Here, "it" means the thing you are doing, and "up" has the meaning of completely . So, **keep it up** mean to continue doing.

[stand-alone phrase]

- You're almost finished with your homework. **Keep it up**.
- You've been late every day. If you **keep it up**, the boss is going to fire you.

193: keep you posted

to continuously inform someone of a situation

In the old days people used to stay connected with the post office system, so when you keep someone posted you keep in contact with them.

[someone] **keeps** [someone] **posted**

- **Keep** me **posted** when Jane arrives. I need to talk to her.
- Carl **kept** everyone **posted** about his trip to China.

194: keep something under your hat

Definition
to keep a secret

Usage Notes
Your head is under your hat and if you **keep something under your hat** you keep it in your head instead of speaking it.

Structure
[someone] **keeps** [something] **under their hat**

Examples
- I have a secret. Promise to **keep it under your hat**.
- Paul **kept the company secret under his hat**.

195: keep your chin up

Definition
to persevere

Usage Notes
If you are discouraged you may hang your head down, but keeping your chin up keeps you in a positive position.

Structure
[stand-alone phrase]

Examples
- I know you are having a tough time, but it'll get better. **Keep your chin up**!
- It's hard to **keep your chin up** when bad things happen.

114

196: keep your eyes peeled

Definition
to watch for something carefully

Usage Notes
When you remove the peel from a fruit, the fruit is open and exposed. So we say **keep your eyes peeled**.

Structure
[someone] **keeps their eyes peeled**

Examples
- Keep your **eyes peeled for the mailman**. I'm expecting a package.
- John said we should **keep our eyes peeled** for a green Chevy. That's his car.

197: keep your head above water

Definition
to continue living in the face of adversity

Usage Notes
If you fell from ship in the ocean, you would need to keep your head above the water in order to survive.

Structure
[someone] **keeps their head above water**

Examples
- It's hard to **keep your head above water** when you don't have a job.
- He spends so much money, how can he **keep his head above water**?

198: kick the habit

Definition
quit a bad habit

Usage Notes
When you kick something you push it away from you strongly, so to **kick the habit** means to get away from a bad habit.

Structure
[someone] **kicks the habit**

Examples
- I'm going to **kick the habit** and stop smoking.
- Tommy used to drink a lot of beer but thankfully he **kicked the habit**.

199: kid around

Definition
to joke with; to not be serious

Usage Notes
Here, "kid" means to make a joke. When you **kid around** you make jokes.

Structure
[someone] **kids around**

Examples
- I like to tell jokes and **kid around**.
- Those boys can be mean when they **kid around**.

200: kill two birds with one stone

to accomplish two things with one action

In the old days people use to hunt birds with stones, so **killing two birds with one stone** was a major accomplishment.

[someone] **kills two birds with one stone**

- We're late for the party. If we go to the card store and the bakery next door, we can **kill two birds with one stone**.
- We can **kill two birds with one stone** if we have a garage sale. We can get rid of stuff and make some money.

201: killer

Terrible; very bad

A killer is a terrible person so something that is a killer is a terrible situation. We use **killer** as an adjective.

killer [something]

- I have a **killer** headache.
- She gave him a **killer** look.

202: last resort

the final chance or solution to a problem

Here, "resort" means a strategy or a course of action, so your last resort is your last course of action to solve a problem.

[something] is a **last resort**

- Let's try to fix the computer and if not, as a **last resort**, we can call someone for help.
- We can invite Dean, but only **as a last resort**. There are better choices for the keynote speech.

203: lay your cards on the table

to speak frankly

At the end of a poker game the players **lay their cards on the table** to frankly show everyone what they have.

[someone] **lays their cards on the table**

- When asked for the truth, Timmy had to **lay his cards on the table** and say he didn't love her.
- I'm going to **lay my cards on the table** and tell you I have no solution to your problem.

204: leadfoot

Definition
to drive too fast

Usage Notes
Lead is a very heavy metal. If you're foot were made of lead it would depress the accelerator in your car very strongly.

Structure
[someone] is / has a **leadfoot**

Examples
- Keith is a **leadfoot**. He drives too fast.
- Winny gets a lot of speeding tickets because she has a **leadfoot**.

205: leave you holding the bag

Definition
to walk away from a bad situation resulting in another person having to bear the responsibility

Usage Notes
If you give your bag to someone and then walk away, you leave them with the responsibility for the bag.

Structure
[someone] **leaves** [someone] **holding the bag**

Examples
- Sorry to **leave you holding the bag**, but I can't stay and help.
- Iris **left Melanie holding the bag** when she skipped the meeting.

206: let sleeping dogs lie

Definition
to not instigate or a dangerous situation

Usage Notes
It's dangerous to wake a sleeping dog, so it is best to allow the dog to continue sleeping.

Structure
[stand-alone phrase]

Examples
- You better not bring that up again. Better to **let sleeping dogs lie**.
- Why don't we **let sleeping dogs lie** and move on to the next subject on the meeeting agenda.

207: let you go

Definition
to end the relationship or employment with someone

Usage Notes
When you **let someone go** you end a relationship with them.

Structure
A person or a company **lets [someone] go**

Examples
- We simply don't have enough work for three people. I'm afraid I have to **let you go**.
- If I find out Frank is cheating on me, I will **let him go**.

208: level with you

to be honest with someone in the face of a negative situation

Level means even or the same so when you level with someone you are honest with them.

[someone] **levels with** [someone]

- **Level with me**, Tim. Did you take the money?
- Barry had to **level with his mom** and say he ate the last cookie.

209: lighten up

don't be so serious about this!

A serious conversation is heavy, so when you **lighten up** the conversation becomes less serious.

[stand-alone phrase]

- Don't be so serious. **Lighten up** and have some fun.
- My mom is so strict. I wish she'd **lighten up**.

210: like a chicken with its head cut off

Definition
to be very disorganized or to act in a disorganized way.

Usage Notes
If you cut off the chicken head its body would walk around in a very disorganized way*.

Yes, I know this is a strange idiom! - MD

Structure
[someone] is like a chicken with its head cut off

Examples
- When Lenny gets stressed out, he is **like a chicken with its head cut off**.
- If you plan your day, you won't need to run **around like a chicken with its head cut off**.

211: like crazy

Definition
terribly; severly

Usage Notes
Here, crazy means very much or severely. This idiom is used as an adverb.

Structure
[something] happens **like crazy**

Examples
- It's raining **like crazy** out there.
- We ran around **like crazy** to get ready for the party.

212: like pulling teeth

Definition
a very difficult and emotional situation

Usage Notes
Having the dentist pull out one of your teeth is very difficult and uncomfortable.

Structure
[something] is **like pulling teeth**

Examples
- It was **like pulling teeth** to get Peter to make a decision about the meeting.
- Getting him ready for school on time was **like pulling teeth**.

213: live it up

Definition
to enjoy

Usage Notes
Here, "it" means the situation, so when you live it up you enjoy it to the fullest amount.

Structure
[someone] **lives it up**

Examples
- It's the weekend, time to **live it up**.
- On my vacation, I'm going to **live it up**, and not worry about anything.

214: live with it

Definition
to reluctantly accept a negative situation

Usage Notes
When you live with something or someone you spend a lot of time with that thing or person and accept that thing or person.

Structure
[someone] lives with it

Examples
- My car is old, but it's all I can afford. I'll have to **just live with it** for now.
- You aren't the only person on earth who still has an iPhone 4. **Live with it**.

215: load off your mind

Definition
an emotionally relieving situation

Usage Notes
A load is a large amount of heavy something. When you have a load off your mind it means that heavy thing is no longer on your mind.

Structure
[something] is a **load off** [someone]'s **mind**

Examples
- My sister is going to watch the baby today. That's a **load off my mind**.
- I'm nervous about my trip, but I packed my suitcase last night. That's a **load off my mind**.

216: loaded

Definition
very drunk

Usage Notes
When a gun is **loaded,** the chambers are completely filled with bullets. So, when a person is **loaded,** their body is completely filled with alcohol.

Structure
[someone] is **loaded**

Examples
- Mary was **loaded** at the party last night.
- Please take my keys, I'm too **loaded** to drive.

217: look forward to

Definition
to think about an upcoming event with pleasure

Usage Notes
Here, forward represents the future. When do you **look forward to** something you think about that future thing with pleasant thoughts.

Structure
[someone] looks forward to [something]

Examples
- By Wednesday, Betsy **looks forward to** the weekend.
- I **look forward to** going to the movies with you.

218: look sharp

Definition
to look stylish or fashionable

Usage Notes
Here, sharp means stylish. When you **look sharp** you look very stylish.

Structure
[someone] **looks sharp**

Examples
- Those new sunglasses make you **look sharp**.
- Justin **looked sharp** in his new suit.

219: lose it

Definition
to become angry or upset

Usage Notes
Here, "it" means your sense of control. When you lose your sense of control you become angry.

Structure
[someone] **loses it**

Examples
- If she doesn't stop talking on her mobil phone, I'm going to **lose it**.
- I **lose it** every time I hear that song. It reminds me of my ex-wife.

220: lose your cool

Definition
to become angry or upset

Usage Notes
When you are angry you're hot, and all of your coolness has left your body.

Structure
[someone] **loses their cool**

Examples
- Terry **lost his cool** when he saw the dent in the fender of his new car.
- Don't **lose your cool**, he's just joking with you.

221: lose your marbles

Definition
to become irrational

Usage Notes
Here, marbles represents your mind. When you **lose your marbles** you lose your mind and becoming irrational.

Structure
[someone] **loses their marbles**

Examples
- Are you kidding? Have you **lost your marbles**?
- Don't **lose your marbles** over that quiz.

222: lose your touch

Definition
to no longer be able to perform as well as before

Usage Notes
This idiom comes from playing the piano. When you play the piano you touch the keys. When you **lose your touch** you're unable to do that.

Structure
[someone] **loses their touch**

Examples
- Ashley can't seem to hit the ball today. She has **lost her touch**.
- I tried really hard to fix my laptop, but nothing worked. I think I have **lost my touch**.

223: lost cause

Definition
a hopeless situation

Usage Notes
A cause is a situation. So, a **lost cause** is a hopeless situation.

Structure
[something] is a **lost cause**

Examples
- I'll never understand geometry. It's a **lost cause**.
- City council won't approve your idea. It's a **lost cause**.

224: lucky dog

Definition
a very lucky person

Usage Notes
Dogs are lucky animals because humans generally treat them very well. So, a **lucky dog** is a person in a very lucky situation

Structure
[someone] is a **lucky dog**

Examples
- You got those tickets for free? Oh, you're a **lucky dog**!
- What a **lucky dog** you are to find that money in the street.

225: make a fortune

Definition
to earn a great deal of money

Usage Notes
A fortune is a great deal of money. When you **make a fortune** it means you earn a great deal of money.

Structure
[someone] **makes a fortune**

Examples
- I'm going to **make a fortune** with this idea.
- George **made a fortune** in the stock market.

226: make do

Definition
to get by in the face of adversity

Usage Notes
When you **make do** you survive in a situation with very few resources.

Structure
[someone] **makes do**

Examples
- We just have $50 until payday, so we have to **make do** with what we have.
- The castaways had to **make do** with whatever washed up on the beach or what they could find on that island.

227: make ends meet

Definition
to be able live or survive each month with just enough money to pay for your expenses

Usage Notes
Each month when the end of the money meets the end of the expenses you **make ends meet**.

Structure
[someone] **makes ends meet**

Examples
- If we reduce our spending, we can **make ends meet**.
- It's hard to **make ends meet** when you're out of work.

228: make a fool of yourself

Definition
to act foolishly

Usage Notes
A fool is a ridiculous person. When you **make a fool of yourself** you act like a ridiculous person.

Structure
[someone] **makes a fool of themselves**

Examples
- Every time you speak about politics, you **make a fool of yourself**. You shouldn't do that at parties!
- If you want to **make a fool of yourself** and wear that ridiculous hat, then that's your choice.

229: make it

Definition
to arrive

Usage Notes
Here, "it" refers to your destination. When you make it, you reach your destination.

Structure
[someone] **makes it**

Examples
- I'll **make it** there tomorrow by five o'clock.
- Despite the snowstorm, Kelly **made it** home.

230: make a living

to earn money from a job

People work in order to live. When you **make a living** you earn money in order to live.

[someone] **makes a living**

- He wasn't rich, but he **made a good living** selling shoes.
- I **make a living** fixing cars.

231: make out (1)

to comprehend

Here, **make out** means to comprehend or understand something

[someone] **makes out** [something]

- It was hard to **make out** what the man was saying because he spoke quietly.
- Sorry, but I couldn't **make out** what you wrote.

232: make out (2)

Definition
to kiss romantically

Usage Notes
Here, **make out** means to kiss romantically.

Structure
[someone] **makes out**

Examples
- Bob's son and his girlfriend were **making out** in the basement.
- You shouldn't **make out** in the classroom!

233: make out (3)

Definition
to result or end up

Usage Notes
Here, **make out** means to result or end up in some certain way.

Structure
[someone] **makes out** a certain way

Examples
- How did you **make out** on your final exam?
- We **made out** well with our presentation.

234: make a pig of yourself

Definition
to eat with poor table manners; to eat excessively

Usage Notes
Pigs are considered to be unclean animals, especially when they eat. If you **make a pig of yourself**, you eat with poor table manners.

Structure
[someone] **makes a pig of themselves**

Examples
- Kip **made a pig of himself** at the buffet.
- Don't **make a pig of yourself**, just take one piece of cake.

235: make sense

Definition
to be understandable

Usage Notes
When something is sensible it's understandable so something that **makes sense** can be understood.

Structure
[something] **makes sense**

Examples
- I have been trying to figure out how to assemble this desk I bought at Kiea, but the instructions don't **make sense**.
- Finally Debby was **making sense**. At first I couldn't understand her point.

236: make time for

Definition
to arrange your schedule for a particular appointment or plan

Usage Notes
When you **make time for** something you arrange your schedule for that.

Structure
[someone] **makes time for** ~

Examples
- You need to always **make time for** some exercise.
- To do well in school, you have to **make time for** homework.

237: make tracks

Definition
to leave for somewhere

Usage Notes
Tracks are footprints, and when someone is walking forward they leave footprints in the ground.

Structure
[someone] **makes tracks**

Examples
- Let's **make tracks** and get out of the office. It's quitting time!
- Right after work, Calvin **makes tracks** to the gym.

238: make up your mind

Definition
to decide

Usage Notes
When you **make up your mind** you decide something.

Structure
[someone] **makes up their mind**

Examples
- I can't **make up my mind** if I want vanilla or chocolate.
- Steven **made up his mind** to become a fireman.

239: make your day

Definition
to pleasanty surprise someone

Usage Notes
When something **makes your day**, it means something causes your day to become wonderful.

Structure
[someone] or [something] **makes** [someone]'s **day**

Examples
- If we don't hit traffic on the highway, it will **make my day**.
- Seeing you smile **makes my day**.

240: make your mouth water

Definition
to stimulate my appetite

Usage Notes
When your appetite is stimulated the inside of your mouth becomes wet. Something that **makes your mouth water** stimulates your appetite.

Structure
[something] **makes** [someone]'s **mouth water**

Examples
- The smell from the bakery **makes my mouth water**.
- It **makes her mouth water** to think of those juicy steaks.

241: mess up

Definition
to make a mistake; to do badly

Usage Notes
A mess is a disorganized or dirty area. When you **mess up**, you miss-handle the situation.

Structure
[someone] **messes up**

Examples
- I **messed up** my exam. I should have studied more.
- If I follow all the instructions, I can't **mess up**.

242: milk something

Definition
to intentionally take more time than is actually required

Usage Notes
It takes a long time and a lot of work to get milk from a cow.

Structure
[someone] **milks something**

Examples
- The construction crew was **milking the job** in order to earn more overtime pay.
- That job should only take an hour. Nick is really **milking that project.**

243: miss the boat

Definition
to lose an opportunity

Usage Notes
In the old days people travel by ship and the departures were infrequent. So if you missed the boat you might have lost an opportunity to travel.

Structure
[someone] **misses the boat**

Examples
- Don't **miss the boat**. You should buy that stock now.
- If you are not paying attention to what the customer is saying, you'll **miss the boat**.

244: nada

Definition
nothing

Usage Notes
Nada is the shortened pronunciation of the phrase "not a thing" - "not a" is often prounounce **nada**.

Structure
[stand-alone phrase]

Examples
- Did you catch any fish? No, **nada**.
- I've got **nada** in my bank account now. I can't wait till payday.

245: nerd vs geek

Definition
a **geek** is a person who is fixated with technology , animation, and/or science fiction. A **nerd** is a **geek** who is anti-social and has very little social interaction.

Usage Notes
See above.

Structure
[someone] is a **nerd** / **geek**

Examples
- **Nerds** are technical , and **geeks** are artistic.
- **Geeks** will talk for hours at a party, **nerds** can't wait to go home.

246: nervous wreck

Definition
a person with a high level of anxiety

Usage Notes
A wreck is something that is badly damaged. So a **nervous wreck** is a person who is very anxious.

Structure
[someone] is a **nervous wreck**

Examples
- The roads are so icy. I'm a **nervous wreck** driving in this storm.
- Every time there is a French test, Sylvie is a **nervous wreck**.

247: nip something in the bud

Definition
to correct a situation before it becomes a problem

Usage Notes
A **bud** is an unopen flower. Nip means to cut. So if you nip the bud you cut the flower before it opens.

Structure
[someone] **nips** [something] **in the bud**

Examples
- You should **nip that bad habit in the bud.**
- The police **nipped that riot in the bud**. Thankfully nobody was injured.

248: no laughing matter

Definition
a serious situation

Usage Notes
A laughing matter is a funny or carefree situation. We always use this idiom in a negative sentence.

Structure
[something] is **no laughing matter**

Examples
- It's **no laughing matter** when someone gets hurt.
- Getting lost in the forest is **no laughing matter**.

249: no matter how you slice it

Definition
regardless of how you look at something

Usage Notes
A pizza is a pizza. Regardless of how the pizza is sliced it's still a pizza.

Structure
[stand-alone phrase]

Examples
- I realize it is cheap, but **no matter how you slice it**, the house is too small.
- There is no way we can do it, **no matter how you slice it**.

250: no strings attached

Definition
without any commitiment

Usage Notes
String or rope can be used to attach things together. When there are **no strings attached** there is no connection.

Structure
[someone] does something with **no strings attached**

Examples
- He gave it to me for free, **no strings attached**.
- The deal has **no strings attached**, so we don't need to sign a contact.

251: no sweat

Definition
no problem

Usage Notes
People sweat when they use their energy. If someone asks you to do something and you don't need to use your energy, you won't sweat.

Structure
[stand-alone phrase]

Examples
- You need help painting the house? I will take care of it, **no sweat**.
- Oh, you'll be late? **No sweat**!

252: no use crying over spilt milk

Definition
worrying about a situation that has happened doesn't solve the problem.

Usage Notes
If someone has spilled milk, getting upset about the spilled milk won't change the situation of the spilled milk.

Structure
[stand-alone phrase]

Examples
- We lost the ball game, **no use crying over spilt milk**.
- **No use crying over spilt milk**. The factory closed, so you'll need to look for another job.

253: no wonder

Definition
the reason is clear and obvious

Usage Notes
Something that is a wonder is unclear and mysterious. When something is **no wonder** it's very clear.

Structure
[something] is **no wonder**

Examples
- **No wonder** the car stalled, we're out of gas.
- It's **no wonder** Tom got the promotion, he worked hard.

254: not have a clue

Definition
to be completely uninformed

Usage Notes
A clue is a hint about something. When someone **doesn't have a clue** it means they know very little or nothing about that situation.

Structure
[someone] does **not have a clue**

Examples
- I **don't have a clue** about to fixing computers.
- They interviewed Frank for six hourse, but he insisted that he **had no clue** where the money went.

255: not long for this world

Definition
near death

Usage Notes
We used not long for this world for both people and objects like electronic or mechanical devices.

Structure
[someone] or [something] is **not long for this world**

Examples
- My car keeps breaking down. It's **not long for this world**.
- Dolly's horse is twenty years old. It's **not long for this world**.

256: not sleep a wink

Definition
to be unable to sleep

Usage Notes
A wink is when you close and open your eye for just a moment. When you do**n't sleep a wink** you're unable to sleep. This idiom is only used in the negative.

Structure
[someone] **does not sleep a wink**

Examples
- I was so nervous about my surgery, I **didn't sleep a wink**.
- We were having so much fun, **no one slept a wink**.

257: nothing to write home about

Definition
no special; ordinary

Usage Notes
In the old days when people traveled or lived away from home they would write letters to their home to inform them of their important news. Where there is **nothing to write home about**, there is nothing special.

Structure
[something] is **nothing to write home about**

Examples
- The movie wasn't **anything to write home about**.
- The restaurant was OK. The meal was **nothing to write home about**.

258: nuts and bolts

Definition
the basic and fundamental objective of something

Usage Notes
Nuts and bolts are the basic components of a structure.

Structure
the nuts and bolts of [something]

Examples
- When you get down to the **nuts and bolts** of it, understanding finance is easy.
- You need to learn the **nuts and bolts** of the business before you make a decision.

259: odds and ends

Definition
miscellaneous items

Usage Notes
Odds and ends are miscellaneous items.

Structure
[stand-alone phrase]

Examples
- All they found in the basement were **odds and ends**.
- He could not find a full set of tools, just some **odds and ends**.

260: off the wall

Definition
unusual & unexpected

Usage Notes
If you hang up a picture on your wall it may fall off unexpectedly. Something that is **off the wall** is unusual and unexpected.

Structure
[someone] or [something] is **off the wall**

Examples
- Ted's **off the wall** idea didn't work and eventually he got fired.
- His **off the wall** comments were very rude.

261: on a shoestring

Definition
on a limited budget

Usage Notes
A shoestring or shoelace is a very inexpensive item.

Structure
[someone] is **on a shoestring**

Examples
- By shopping wisely, the family lived **on a shoestring**.
- Mary planned the party **on a shoestring**, and it was fabulous.

262: on deck

ready for your turn

In baseball, the next batter who is awaiting his turn is referred to as the **on deck** batter.

[someone] is **on deck**

- Fred is the next speaker; he's **on deck**.
- With the storm approaching, the rescue team was **on deck**.

263: on edge

nervous

If you stood on the edge of a mountain or cliff you would be very nervous.

[someone] is **on edge**

- Dave has been **on edge** since he went to the doctor.
- You seem **on edge** today. Is something wrong?

264: on standby

to wait to be given an assignment

Before the actor goes onto the stage, he needs to stand by the stage and wait for his cue.

[someone] is **on standby**

- I'm **on standby** this weekend in case they need extra help at work.
- Donna is **on standby** for the next flight to New York.

265: on the brink

very near or close to a bad situation

A brink is the edge of a high cliff. When you are on the brink you are very close to a bad situation.

[someone] is **on the brink**

- The team was **on the brink** of defeat when they finally made their comeback.
- The scientist was **on the brink** of losing his eyesight when his experiment exploded.

266: on the fence

Definition
undecided

Usage Notes
A fence divides two places. When you are **on the fence** you can go to either side.

Structure
[someone] is **on the fence**

Examples
- I'm **on the fence** about buying that car. I like it, but I don't love it.
- Have you made up your mind, or are you still **on the fence**?

267: on the go

Definition
very busy

Usage Notes
Here, "go" refers to movement. When you are **on the go** you're very busy.

Structure
[someone] is **on the go**

Examples
- Jim never stops. He's always **on the go**.
- My calendar is full today. I'll be **on the go** until 5PM.

268: on the job

Working; while working

When you are **on the job** you are working.

[someone] does something **on the job**

- I learned how to be a carpenter **on the job**.
- With Harry **on the job**, I knew it would be done right.

269: on the run

escaping from the police

Someone who is **on the run** is escaping, usually from the police.

[someone] is **on the run**

- That guy was **on the run** for ten years before the police caught him.
- The bank robbers were **on the run** from the police.

270: on thin ice

Definition
facing someone's anger or displeasure

Usage Notes
This idiom comes from ice skating. If the ice is thin it is a precarious situation. We use **on thin ice with** when the direct object is used.

Structure
[someone] is **on thin ice**

Examples
- Ever since the argument, Bill was **on thin ice** with Glenda.
- Be careful with you say, you're **on thin ice** with mom.

271: on the take

Definition
receiving illegal payments in return for favors

Usage Notes
Someone who is **on the take** is taking illegal payments.

Structure
[someone] is **on the take**

Examples
- Henry always used the same supplier because he was **on the take**.
- The corrupt politicians were **on the take**. That's how they got so much campaign money.

272: onto something

Definition
realizing the solution

Usage Notes
When you are **onto something** you finally realize it.

Structure
[someone] is **onto something**

Examples
- That's a great idea! You're really **onto something**.
- The fingerprints told the police they were **onto something**.

273: open-minded

Definition
willing to listen to other's opinions

Usage Notes
A person who is **open-minded** is willing to listen to others opinions.

Structure
[someone] is **open-minded**

Examples
- Greg is **open-minded** about most issues except politics.
- I can't be **open-minded** when you speak like that.

274: out loud

Definition
using your voice

Usage Notes
When you speak **out loud** the sound comes out of your mouth loudly.

Structure
[someone] does something **out loud**

Examples
- She made a wish **out loud**, hoping someone would hear it.
- Sometimes it's better to not say things **out loud**.

275: out of it

Definition
tired and listless

Usage Notes
Here, "it" means your usual feeling. When you are **out of it** you don't feel the way you usually feel.

Structure
[someone] is **out of it**

Examples
- My allergies are making me feel **out of it** today.
- I stayed out way too late last night. I'm **out of it** this morning.

276: out of sorts

Definition
physically uncomfortable

Usage Notes
When you feel **out of sorts** you feel physically uncomfortable.

Structure
[someone] is **out of sorts**

Examples
- My stomach is **out of sorts** after eating that chili.
- Barry felt **out of sorts** in his new apartment.

277: out of the picture

Definition
no longer considered or thought about

Usage Notes
Someone or something who is out **of the picture** is no longer being considered. They are no longer in the photo.

Structure
[someone] or [something] is **out of the picture**

Examples
- Beth and I are no longer dating. She's **out of the picture**.
- That house is **out of the picture**, it's too expensive.

278: out of the woods

Definition
no longer in a negative situation

Usage Notes
It's very easy to get lost in the woods. When you are **out of the woods** you are no longer in a bad situation.

Structure
[someone] is **out of the woods**

Examples
- Now that the storm is over, I think we're **out of the woods**.
- We paid off the loan, but we're not **out of the woods** yet.

279: out of work

Definition
unemployed

Usage Notes
Here, "out" means away from. When you are **out of work** you don't have a job.

Structure
[someone] is **out of work**

Examples
- Tom lost his job. He's **out of work**.
- When the factory closed down, the whole town was **out of work**.

280: over the hill

Definition
too old; past your prime of life

Usage Notes
Here, "the hill" represents the middle of someone's life. When you are **over the hill** you are past your prime.

Structure
[someone] is **over the hill**

Examples
- Grandpa is **over the hill**. he just watches TV all day in bed.
- Today, being 40 years old is considered **over the hill** in some cultures.

281: over your head

Definition
beyond your mental capacity or ability

Usage Notes
You use your head to understand something. When something is **over your head** you are unable to understand it.

Structure
[something] is **over** [someone]'s **head**

Examples
- I don't know how to do this. It's way **over my head**.
- That math problem is **over my head**, so I can't help you.

282: pass out

Definition
to faint

Usage Notes
Your mind can **pass out** of consciousness and into unconsciousness.

Structure
[someone] **passes out**

Examples
- If I don't get some fresh air, I'll **pass out**.
- After you drink too much, you will **pass out**.

283: pay your dues

Definition
as a new employee to accept doing jobs or tasks that may not be interesting, but are essential for a career.

Usage Notes
The money that you pay to become a member of a club is called "dues." **Paying your dues** is the negative aspect of being in the club.

Structure
[someone] **pay's their dues**

Examples
- You can't start working in a company at the top management level, you have to **pay your dues** first.
- If you want respect in this industry, be prepared to **pay your dues** and work hard.

284: pick up the pace

Definition
to move faster

Usage Notes
Here, pick up means to accelerate. When you **pick up the pace** you move faster.

Structure
[someone] **picks up the pace**

Examples
- We're late! We had better **pick up the pace**.
- We have to **pick up the pace** if we want to catch up with them.

285: piece of your mind

Definition
your opinion

Usage Notes
Your opinion lies in one section of your mind. When you give someone a **piece of your mind** you give them your opinion. Generally we use this when we are upset.

Structure
[someone] gives someone a **piece of their mind**

Examples
- I am so annoyed at Tina. I'm going to give her a **piece of my mind**.
- Even if he didn't ask for my advice, I am gong to give him a **piece of my mind**.

286: pig out

Definition
to over eat

Usage Notes
Pigs like to eat a lot of food. When you **pig out** you overeat. Use **pig out on** when a direct object is used.

Structure
[someone] **pigs out**

Examples
- I'm going to **pig out** on those donuts.
- Everyone at the buffet came to **pig out**.

287: pitch in

Definition
to help, to assist

Usage Notes
When you **pitch in**, you help or assist someone with something.

Structure
[someone] **pitches in**

Examples
- The whole town **pitched in** to rebuild the school after the storm.
- If everyone **pitches in**, the job will go faster.

288: play along

Definition
to do something unwillingly, but in order to avoid conflict

Usage Notes
An actor in a play is acting. When you **play along**, you become like an actor in the situation.

Structure
[someone] **plays along**

Examples
- You don't have to agree with me, just **play along**.
- If you **play along** with the robber, no one will get hurt.

289: plug away

Definition
to work slowly but steadily

Usage Notes
When you **plug away** at something you work slowly but steadily to finish it.

Structure
[someone] **plugs away**

Examples
- Mel continued to **plug away** at his homework.
- If you **plug away** at it, you'll eventually finish.

290: plug something

Definition
to promote

Usage Notes
I'll plug is inserted into a receptacle. When you plug in something, you insert an advertisement for that thing.

Structure
[someone] **plugs** something

Examples
- The actor was on the talk show to **plug** his new movie.
- Advertisements are a good way to **plug** a new beauty product.

291: pound the pavement

Definition
to make a lot of effort to succeed

Usage Notes
The pavement is the street. Pound means to walk with very heavy feet. Someone who **pounds the pavement** makes a lot of effort in order to succeed.

Structure
[someone] **pounds the pavement**

Examples
- It used to be that to find a job, you had to **pound the pavement**.
- The demonstrators **pounded the pavement** all the way to city hall.

292: pull an all-nighter

Definition
to something (like work, study, hang out) over midnight and until the early morning

Usage Notes
All night means from sundown to sun up. When you **pull an all-nighter**, you work or study through the night until dawn.

Structure
[someone] **pulls an all-nighter**

Examples
- I had to **pull an all-nighter** to finish this report.
- Dave **pulled an all-nighter** before the big exam.

293: pull punches

Definition
In the negative, to speak directly and less forcefuly than what the listener may expect.

Usage Notes
This idiom is usually used in a negative sentence. When you don't **pull punches** you speak directly,

Structure
[someone] **pulls punches**

Examples
- I'm going to be honest with you and **pull no punches**. I think your idea is not good.
- **Don't pull any punches**, doctor. How bad is my situation?

294: pull your leg

Definition
to joke or kid someone

Usage Notes
When someone **pulls your leg** they are not being serious with you.

Structure
[someone] **pulls** [someone]'s **leg**

Examples
- Is this a joke?Are you **pulling my leg**? Did I really win $1,000,000?
- On April Fool's Day, it's fun to **pull someone's leg**.

295: pull through

Definition
to recover; to survive an ordeal

Usage Notes
When someone **pulls through** they recover from an illness or survive a difficult situation.

Structure
[someone] **pulls through**

Examples
- It looks like Jill will **pull through** after her surgery.
- After these tough economic times, many people are having trouble **pulling through**.

296: pull yourself together

Definition
to gain composure

Usage Notes
When you lose composure, we say that you fall apart. When you **pull yourself together**, you gain composure again.

Structure
[someone] **pulls themselves together**

Examples
- After receiving the bad news, Jim had to **pull himself together** and figure out what to do.
- Stop crying, and try to **pull yourself together**. Everything is going to be ok.

297: punch it

Definition
to depress the car's accelerator pedal strongly in order to go faster.

Usage Notes
Here, "it" means the accelerator pedal of your car. When you punch it with your foot you accelerate the car.

Structure
[someone] **punches it**

Examples
- To get the car up this big hill, you'll need to **punch it**.
- **Punch it**! Let's get out of here. The police are coming.

298: put all your eggs in one basket

Definition
to rely on only one solution or idea, ignoring other possibilities

Usage Notes
If you need to move several eggs, it could be risky to carry them in one basket.

Structure
[someone] **puts all of their eggs in one basket**

Examples
- You should consider both stocks and bonds. You don't want to **put all your eggs in one basket**.
- Tom is working on the project alone. **I don't want to put all my eggs in one basket**, let's ask Phil to help him.

299: put you on

Definition
to not speak seriously

Usage Notes
When you **put someone on** your not speaking seriously to that person.

Structure
[someone] **puts** [someone] **on**

Examples
- That can't be true! You're **putting me on**.
- Where you **putting me on** when you told me that?.

300: put something on the back burner

Definition
to give something a very low priority

Usage Notes
When cooking, soups and sauces can be on the back burner of the stove because they don't require your attention as much as the food cooking in a frypan does.

Structure
[someone] puts something on the back burner

Examples
- This just came in. I have to **put what I was doing on the back burner**.
- The boss said we should **put everything else on the back burner** and work on the marketing plan.

301: put up with

Definition
to endure

Usage Notes
When you **put up** with something you endure an unpleasant situation.

Structure
[someone] **puts up with** [something]

Examples
- I can't **put up with** the noise! Please close the window.
- Jenny said she **can't put up** with her husband's drinking problem anymore.

302: put your foot in your mouth

Definition
to embarrass yourself

Usage Notes
Sometimes babies put their foot in their mouth. We think that's cute. If an adult did that, such behavior would be very embarrassing.

Structure
[someone] **puts their foot in their mouth**

Examples
- I shouldn't have said that. I **really put my foot in my mouth**.
- Bill **put his foot in his mouth** when he mispronounced the CEO's name at the meeting.

303: rain on your parade

Definition
to give someone disappointing news

Usage Notes
A rain storm during the parade would be disappointing for the people marching and the spectators.

Structure
[someone] **rains on** [someone]'s **parade**

Examples
- Steve **rained** on Mary's **parade** when he told her he was leaving her.
- Nothing can **rain on my parade** because I'm in a great mood today.

168

304: rant and rave

Definition
to complain angrily

Usage Notes
Rant means to speak passionately for a long time and rave means to speak angrily.

Structure
[someone] **rants and raves**

Examples
- Calm down, no need to **rant and rave**. Now calmly tell me what happened
- The boss was **ranting and raving** for two hours about the poor sales results.

305: rest assured

Definition
don't worry

Usage Notes
Assure means to speak in a way that eliminates someone's doubts. When you have no doubts you don't worry and you can rest well.

Structure
[stand-alone phrase]

Examples
- **Rest assured**, I'm here to help you anytime.
- You can **rest assured**, we'll find the man who robbed the bank.

306: ride his coattails

Definition
have success because of another's success

Usage Notes
The back of a jacket is also known as a coattail. When you **ride someone's coattails** you have success, but only because they had success.

Structure
[someone] **rides** [someone]'s **coattails**

Examples
- The senator won re-election **riding on the coattails** of the President's easy victory.
- Jack got the promotion **riding on Victor's coattails**.

307: right on the money

Definition
quite correct

Usage Notes
When you are idea or speaking is exactly correct we say that you are right on the money. A person or a person's idea can be right on the money.

Structure
[someone] or [something] is **right on the money**

Examples
- Vincent's idea is **right on the money** again. He's a genius.
- Her choice of color was **right on the money**. The living room looks great!

170

308: right-hand man

an invaluable assistant

For right-handed people everything is done with the right-hand. So it's very useful. Your **right-hand man** is your invaluable assistant.

[someone] is [someone]'s **right-hand man**

- I depend on Steve for good advice. He is my **right-hand man**.
- As the boss' **right-hand man**, Dave had to be on call night and day.

309: rip off

an expensive price

We use this idiom as a noun. When something is a rip off, the price is too expensive.

[something] is a **rip off**

- $500 for that carpet is a **rip off**. I'm not buying it.
- I bought a beer at the stadium, but at $15 a bottle, it was a **rip off**.

310: rip someone off

Definition
to rob or cheat someone

Usage Notes
When someone **rips you off**, they cheap or overcharge you.

Structure
[someone] **rips** [someone] **off** or **rips off** [someone]

Examples
- He wanted so much money for that piece of junk. He was trying to **rip me off**.
- The street vendor **ripped me off** charging $5 for a bottle of water!

311: rock the boat

Definition
to disturb a stable situation

Usage Notes
If you stand up in a small boat the boat will rock from side to side. In other words, the boat will become unstable.

Structure
[someone] **rocks the boat**

Examples
- Please, don't **rock the boat**. We have had successful sales with the current website. I don't want to change it now.
- Victor **rocked the boat** at the meeting when he announced his retirement.

172

312: rolling in dough

wealthy

Here, "dough" is a slang word for me money. If you have enough money to spread on the floor and then roll around on top of it, you must be very wealthy.

[someone] is **rolling in dough**

- Ever since Howie won the lottery, he's been **rolling in dough**.
- After getting promoted to director, I'm **rolling in dough**.

313: save the day

to do something that helps someone who is in a tight situation

If you **save the day**, you do something that rescues another person from a difficult situation.

[someone] or [something] **saves the day**

- In the movie, the hero arrived to **save the day**.
- The repairman fixed the freezer and **saved the day**.

314: second nature

Definition
something that is natural to do because you've done it many times before

Usage Notes
When you are very good at doing something because you have done it many times before, we say that thing is **second nature** to you.

Structure
[something] is **second nature** to [someone]

Examples
- I've been cooking this soup my whole life. It's **second nature** to me.
- Bill walked across the tightrope like it was **second nature** to him.

315: second wind

Definition
a refreshing feeling

Usage Notes
A **second wind** is the refreshing feeling that you get after a nap or a shower, etc.

Structure
[something] gives [someone] a **second wind**

Examples
- I feel refreshed after my nap. I got a **second wind**.
- I was exhausted before, but I just got my **second wind**. Let's keep going.

174

316: sell like hotcakes

Definition
sell well; be a good selling product

Usage Notes
In the old days, hotcakes were very popular snacks so it was very easy to sell them.

Structure
[something] **sells like hotcakes**

Examples
- I guarantee these cars will **sell like hotcakes**.
- After people see the movie stars wearing these shoes, they will **sell like hotcakes**.

317: set the record straight

Definition
to make the circumstances clear

Usage Notes
It is easy to see when something is straight. When you **set the record straigh**t, you remove any misunderstanding.

Structure
[someone] **sets the record straight**

Examples
- Let me **set the record straight**; I was not there at the time.
- In order to **set the record straight.** Akira gave his side of the story.

318: shake in your boots

to be nervous

When you are nervous your body shakes. When you shake in your boots, it means you're very nervous.

[someone] **shakes in their boots**

- That scary movie made me **shake in my boots**
- I **shake in my boots** every time the teacher calls on me to answer a question.

319: shell out

to pay too much; to pay unwillingly

We have an image that in the old days, sea shells were used as currency. When you shell out money you pay too much.

[someone] **shells out** money for ~

- Bill had to **shell out** $100 for the tickets.
- Every time I see him, I have to **shell out** some money for something. He never offers to pay.

320: shot in the dark

Definition
a complete guess

Usage Notes
If you shoot a gun in complete darkness, you could only guess as to where the bullet will go.

Structure
[something] is a **shot in the dark**

Examples
- It's a **shot in the dark**, but I think if you connect the blue wire to the green wire, the engine should work.
- This is our last chance, and it's a **shot in the dark**, but I think it will be ok.

321: shut up

Definition
stop talking

Usage Notes
Shut means close, specifically to close your mouth. When you tell someone to shut up, you are telling them to stop talking. We usually use **shut up** when we are angry; it's a bit strong and direct.

Structure
[stand-alone phrase]

Examples
- **Please shut up**! I need some quiet so I can study.
- Ask people to speak softly. Saying **shut up** is a bit rude.

322: sit tight

Definition
wait patiently

Usage Notes
When people are impatient they tend to move their body and fidget. When you **sit tight** you wait patiently.

Structure
[someone] **sits tight**

Examples
- I'll get in touch as soon as I can, so **sit tight** and wait for my call.
- The weather will clear up soon. Let's just **sit tight** for a while.

323: slack off

Definition
to act lazily

Usage Notes
Slack is used to describe a rope which is not tight, and thus, not working to its fullest potential.

Structure
[someone] **slacks off**

Examples
- Students tend to **slack off** at the end of the school year.
- If you **slack off** now, we won't finish the project on time.

324: smash-hit

Definition
a very big hit movie, book, song, etc.

Usage Notes
Smash means to break. A movie or song the breaks sales records is known as a **smash-hit**.

Structure
[something] is a **smash-hit**

Examples
- The new album was a **smash-hit**.
- People were standing in line for several hours to see that **smash-hit** film.

325: spaced out

Definition
to be disoriented or unaware of your surroundings, usually from drugs or medicine

Usage Notes
Some drugs can give people of feeling that they're floating in space.

Structure
[someone] is **spaced out**

Examples
- This medicine makes me feel **spaced out**.
- I am too **spaced out** to drive. Can you drive me home?

326: spill the beans

Definition
to reveal a secret

Usage Notes
Here, beans represents secret information. If you **spill the beans**, the secret information will be revealed.

Structure
[someone] **spills the beans**

Examples
- Please don't **spill the beans** about the surprise party.
- I promise not to tell anyone. I won't be the one to **spill the beans**.

327: spring for

Definition
to pay for

Usage Notes
When you **spring for** something you pay, and often this has the nuance that your paying is unexpected.

Structure
[someone] **springs for** [something]

Examples
- It was so nice of Ken to **spring for** lunch.
- I think I'm going to **spring for** a new watch.

328: square up

Definition
to settle your debts

Usage Notes
A square has four equal sides. When you **square up** you settle your debts and you and the other side are even.

Structure
[someone] **squares up**

Examples
- How much do I owe you? Let's **square up** the bill.
- Your share of the bill is $25. Paying that will **square** everything **up**.

329: steal

Definition
a good bargain

Usage Notes
If you **steal** something you get it without paying money. Something that is **a steal** is a very good bargain.

Structure
[something] is **a steal**

Examples
- I've never seen a price this low for these headphones. It's **a steal**!
- Do you like my watch? It was **a steal**. I paid just $25 for it.

330: stick to your guns

Definition
be unwaivering in your opinion

Usage Notes
In the old days the only dependable things a cowboy had were his guns, and he used his guns to show his strong opinion.

Structure
[someone] **sticks to their guns**

Examples
- I'm going to **stick to my guns** and not change my mind. You need to do the job, not me!
- Even though Candice was wrong, she chose to **stick to her guns**.

331: stick-in-the-mud

Definition
a dull, boring, or uncooperative person

Usage Notes
If you put a stick in mud it's very difficult to move that stick. It will probably just stay there doing nothing. So, **a stick-in-the-mud** is a dull, boring, or uncooperative person.

Structure
[someone] is **a stick-in-the-mud**

Examples
- Robert is no fun. He's **a stick-in-the-mud**.
- Dan never chages his habits. That old **stick-in-the-mud** is in bed by 8pm every night!

332: strapped (for cash)

Definition
having a shortage of cash

Usage Notes
Strapped gives us the image that someone is tied down and can't move. Without money, you're strapped. You can **be strapped** or **strapped for cash**.

Structure
[someone] is **strapped**

Examples
- Can you lend me $20? I'm **strapped** today.
- I didn't get paid today. I'm a little strapped for cash.

333: stressed out

Definition
feeling very stressed

Usage Notes
When you are feeling stressed out you're very stressed.

Structure
[someone] is **stressed out**

Examples
- My blood test was last week. I'm **stressed out** waiting for the doctor to call with the results.
- Whenever I'm stressed out I listen to Mozart to relax.

334: stretch the truth

Definition
to speak somewhat dishonestly

Usage Notes
If you take something that is true and **stretch the truth**, you are not exactly speaking honestly.

Structure
[someone] **stretches the truth**

Examples
- Bill **stretched the truth** when he said he went to the library. He dropped off books there, but then spent the rest of the time in the bar.
- Politicians often **stretch the truth** to get your vote.

335: strike it rich

Definition
to become wealthy

Usage Notes
Strike means to hit. When you **strike it rich** you become very wealthy.

Structure
[someone] **strikes it rich**

Examples
- You can **strike it rich** if you win the lottery.
- I think I am going to **strike it rich** with my new invention.

336: suck it up

to deal with and accept adversity

Here, "it" means your breath. When you suck in your breath, you don't speak.

[someone] **sucks it up**

- Stop complaining and **suck it up**. You can have a cookie after dinner.
- I've been avoiding going to the dentist for a few weeks now, but the pain in my tooth is getting worse. I think I need to **suck it up** and have it checked.

337: sure thing

a certainly successful venture

Something that is a **sure thing** will certainly have success.

[something] is a **sure thing**

- Making money by selling goods on eBay was a **sure thing** in the early 2000's
- That horse is a **sure thing** to win the race this afternoon. You should bet on it.

338: sweat it

Definition
to worry

Usage Notes
People sweat when they are nervous about something. We often tell someone, "Don't **sweat it**" when we want to encourge them to not be nervous about something.

Structure
[someone] **sweats it**

Examples
- I know you're nervous about your presentation. Don't **sweat it**. You'll do fine!
- Don't **sweat it**. The exam is not as difficult as you may think.

339: sweep something under the rug

Definition
to ignore a problem

Usage Notes
If there is something on your floor and you sweep that under the rug, you no longer see it.

Structure
[someone] **sweeps something under the rug**

Examples
- The school tried to **sweep the scandal under the rug**, but somehow the news media found out.
- You can't just **sweep this under the rug**. The boss will eventually know that you lost the deal.

340: sweet tooth

Definition
have a love for sweets, deserts, etc

Usage Notes
When you have a **sweet tooth** you love sweets and desserts very much.

Structure
[someone] has a **sweet tooth**

Examples
- I have a **sweet tooth**, so I like to eat candy.
- This dessert is just what my **sweet tooth** was craving.

341: take in

Definition
to see a movie / to order food to go and eat it at home

Usage Notes
Take in has two meanings. (1) When you **take in** a movie or a show you go to see the show. (2) You can **take in** food, in other words, have food to go from a restaurant.

Structure
[someone] takes in [something]

Examples
- (1) Let's go **take in** that new action film. It looks exciting.
- (2) I don't feel like going out tonight or cooking. Let's just **take in** some Chinese food and watch TV.

342: take it easy

Definition
goodbye; relax

Usage Notes
Take it easy has two meanings. (1) **Take it easy** is used as a standalone phrase that means goodbye. (2) **Take it easy** is also used to mean, "please relax."

Structure
[stand-alone phrase]

Examples
- (1) Thanks for visiting! **Take it easy**, and I'll see you soon.
- (2) I know that's bad news George, but try to **take it easy**. Getting angry won't change the situation.

343: take sides

Definition
to favor one person's opinion over another's

Usage Notes
Here, "side" means one person's opinion. If there are two people with different opinions and you favor one of those opinions, you **take sides**.

Structure
[someone] **takes sides**

Examples
- Mary didn't want to **take sides** in the argument.
- It's easy to **take sides**. Either you think he's right or wrong.

344: take something by storm

to be very popular in a short period of time

A storm can have a lot of excitement. We usually use this idiom when we talk about things that are popular in pop-culture, like pop singers, movies, TV shows, etc.

[something] **takes** [someone] **by storm**

- The new rock band **took the country by storm**.
- Yuki's designs are becoming so popular. Soon, they will **take the jewelry world by storm**.

345: talk into

to convince

If you want to convince somebody of something you probably need to talk to them a lot. So, when you **talk someone into something** you convince them.

[someone] **talks** [someone] **into** [something]

- **You talked me into** eating that the last slice of chocolate cake and now my stomache hurts.
- It took two hours, but the salesman **talked Ralph into** buying the car.

346: tell off

Definition
to scold

Usage Notes
When you **tell someone off** you scold and reprimand them.

Structure
[someone] **tells off** [someone]

Examples
- I can't believe she told the boss that I was thinking of quitting. I'm going to tell **her off** for doing that.
- You should never **tell off** anyone who has a higher position that you do in the company.

347: things are looking up

Definition
the situation is improving

Usage Notes
When someone is in a difficult situation they tend to look down. So when **things are looking up** the situation is improving.

Structure
[stand-alone phrase]

Examples
- Eddie finally got a job with the phone company. **Things are looking up** for him.
- **Things are looking up** for Lee since he moved to Pennsylvania. He got a good job, an nice house,and a new girlfriend.

348: think straight

to think rationally or reasonably

Usage Notes
When you **think straight** you think rationally or reasonably. This idiom is generally used in a negative sentence, but can be used in a positive one as well.

Structure
[someone] **thinks straight**

Examples
- I'm so nervous about my job interview, I can't **think straight**. I need to relax a bit.
- The elevator hasn't moved in 10 minutes. Give me a moment to **think straight** and I'll find a solution.

349: throw in the towel

Definition
to give up; to quit

Usage Notes
This idiom comes from the sport of boxing. When a boxer gives up the match, they throw their towel into the middle of the boxing ring.

Structure
[someone] **throws in the towel**

Examples
- I can't do this anymore. I'm going to **throw in the towel**.
- After years of frustration with her boss, Jill **threw in the towel**, quit the job and moved to Florida.

350: tied up

Definition
busy; deeply involved in something.

Usage Notes
If you are busy doing something you can do something else.
It is as if you were tied to that task with rope. You can be
tied up in a situation or **tied up with** a task.

Structure
[someone] is **tied up**

Examples
- I came to the office late because I was **tied up in** traffic for an hour.
- I can't go to the bar today because I'm **tied up with** work.

351: to die for

Definition
excellent; great; wonderful

Usage Notes
There might be something that you love so much you would
be willing to die in order to get.

Structure
[something] is **to die for**

Examples
- Kelly thought that the dress she saw in the shop window was **to die for**.
- The pizza in that restaurant is **to die for**. You should try it!

352: top dollar

Definition
a high price

Usage Notes
The highest point is the top, so when you pay **top dollar** for something you pay very high price for it.

Structure
[something] is **top dollar** / [someone] pays **top dollar** for [something] / [someone] charges **top dollar**

Examples
- I paid **top dollar** for this iPad. Apple never has a sale.
- I don't like shopping there because they charge **top dollar** for everything.

353: turn in

Definition
go to bed

Usage Notes
Sometimes when people go to bed they turn their body to one side.

Structure
[someone] **turns in**

Examples
- I'm so tired; I think I'll **turn in** early tonight.
  I usually **turn in** around 11pm because I need to get up at 6:15am.

354: turn off / turn on

Definition
turn off means repulsive; **turn on** means attractive

Usage Notes
Someone or something that is a **turn off** repulses you. On the other hand, someone or something that is a **turn on** attracts you.

Structure
[someone] or [something] is a **turn off / turn on**

Examples
- Frank's style of speaking is a **turn off**. No wonder he's not a successful salesperson.
- The way Yumi dresses is a **turn on**. She's so attractive.

355: turn up the heat

Definition
to put pressure on someone

Usage Notes
If someone was close to a fire, and the fire became hotter, that would cause them to take action.

Structure
[someone] **turns up the heat**

Examples
- My boss is **turning up the heat** to get this project finished.
- I'm going to have to **turn up the heat** to get the landlord to fix the air conditioner.

194

356: twist your arm

Definition
to strongly pursuade

Usage Notes
In the old days in order to put pressure on someone, the strong guy would inflict pain on them by **twisting their arm**.

Structure
[someone] **twists** [someone]'s **arm**

Examples
- You don't have to **twist my arm**, I'll go with you.
- I had to **twist Leo's arm**, but finally he agreed to go to the beach with me.

357: underway

Definition
in progress

Usage Notes
This idiom comes from sailing. When the ship is **underway** it is in progress and moving toward its destination

Structure
[something] is **underway**

Examples
- The construction on my new house is finally **underway**.
- The new marketing campaign is **underway** and we are getting good results with it.

358: up a creek (without a paddle)

Definition
in a bad or unfortunate situation

Usage Notes
If you work in a boat on a river and you lost the ore or paddle, you would be in a bad situation. This idiom is a short form of the idiom, **up a creek without a paddle**.

Structure
[someone] is **up a creek**

Examples
- I'm **up a creek** without my cell phone. I'm so upset that I lost it
- Tom forgot his keys. He's **up a creek** until someone opens the door.

359: up in arms

Definition
upset and angry

Usage Notes
When you are **up in arms** you are very upset and angry. We use **up in arms over** when a direct object is used.

Structure
[someone] is **up in arms**

Examples
- Relax. No need to get all **up in arms** about the situation.
- The people were **up in arms** over the tax increase.

360: water under the bridge

Definition
something that is no longer relavent

Usage Notes
When water passes under a bridge it is a situation that can't be changed.

Structure
[something] is **water under the bridge**

Examples
- All of the negotiations are finally **water under the bridge**. I am so glad we got the signed contract.
- The old disagreements they had are just **water under the bridge**. They are still close friends.

361: weather the storm

Definition
to endure or survive a difficult period

Usage Notes
This idiom comes from sailing. When a ship waits in a port for a storm to pass, we say that the ship is **weathering the storm**.

Structure
[someone] **weathers the storm**

Examples
- With some savings in the bank, we can **weather the storm** until the layoff is over.
- Because our love is so strong, we can always **weather the storm**.

362: well-off

Definition
wealthy

Usage Notes
A person who is **well-off** is very wealthy.

Structure
[someone] is **well-off**

Examples
- Lucy and her husband are **well-off**. He's a doctor and she is a lawyer.
- All of the customers in that expensive restaurant seem to be **well-off**.

363: wine and dine

Definition
to entertain

Usage Notes
When you **wine and dine** someone you entertain them at a restaurant.

Structure
[someone] **wines and dines** [someone]

Examples
- The businessman **wined and dined** the new client.
- You should **wine and dine** your date to make her feel special.

364: wing it

Definition
to do something without prior preparation

Usage Notes
Here, "it" means a task. When you **wing it** you do that task without the prior preparation.

Structure
[someone] **wings it**

Examples
- The boss just asked me to give a presentation. Since I didn't prepare anything, I have to **wing it**.
- If you don't remember the words to the song, just **wing it**.

365: wiped out

Definition
mentally and physically exhausted

Usage Notes
When you are **wiped out** you are mentally and physically exhausted.

Structure
[someone] is **wiped out**

Examples
- I went to bed so late last night. That's why I'm **wiped out** today.
- Fred was **wiped out** after his karate class.

366: wired

Definition
very alert, usually from caffiene or excitement

Usage Notes
Someone who is **wired** is very alert, as if they had a lot of electrical energy from wires.

Structure
[someone] is **wired**

Examples
- I drank so much coffee. I'm **wired**.
- The teenagers were **wired** listening to their favorte singer at the concert.

367: wolf down

Definition
to eat quickly

Usage Notes
A wolf can eat food very quickly. When you **wolf something down** you eat it very quickly.

Structure
[someone] **wolfs down** [something]

Examples
- I'm so hungry, I could **wolf down** that whole pizza.
- After the ball game, Tony **wolfed down** four hamburgers.

368: work your tail off

Definition
to work very hard

Usage Notes
Dogs used to be used for working on a farm. People would say that the dog is working so hard that his tail will fall off.

Structure
[someone] **works their tail off**

Examples
- I **worked my tail off** to get this report finished on time for the meeting.
- Sasha **worked her tail off** to get the promotion.

Congratulations!

You've reached the end of the book and have probably discovered I've actually put 368 Idioms here! I hope you enjoyed my little surprise! Thanks again for studying with me!

Other books by Michael DiGiacomo, MBA

Available in eBook and Paperback

For more information, visit

myhappyenglish.com

Made in the USA
Monee, IL
22 August 2021

76277732R00115